LOVE MAGNET

LOVE MAGNET

GET OFF THE DATING ROLLERCOASTER
AND ATTRACT THE LOVE YOU DESERVE

DR. MORGAN ANDERSON

HOUNDSTOOTH
PRESS

LOVE MAGNET
Get Off the Dating Rollercoaster and Attract the Love You Deserve

FIRST EDITION

ISBN   978-1-5445-3659-0 *Hardcover*
       978-1-5445-3660-6 *Paperback*
       978-1-5445-3661-3 *Ebook*

For Anthony Lombardi

"Love is the only sane and satisfactory answer to the problem of human existence."

—ERICH FROMM

CONTENTS

NOTE TO THE READER

This book is meant for whoever finds themselves reading it. Regardless of the unique intersections of identity that make you "you," my hope is that you know these words are meant for all. While I write speaking to a female persona, these words serve you no matter your gender identity, race, or sexual orientation.

INTRODUCTION

COMFORT ZONE QUICKSAND

One cold autumn afternoon in the pouring rain, I found myself sprinting down a street in cork wedges, flailing my arms, and screaming "Wait!" I was chasing after a Pepsi delivery truck.

How on earth did this situation come about, you ask? One answer: my beliefs. I quite literally chased after a Pepsi truck because I believed that *love was unavailable to me.* Just two weeks earlier, while salsa dancing and drinking ice cold Coronas at a dive bar, I had fallen in love. His name was Ricardo, and the second our eyes locked, I took a sharp breath in and felt my heart pounding so loud I was afraid others would hear it. He was tall, dark, and deliciously handsome. The moment I saw him, I felt intoxicated by his presence. We had a whirlwind forty-eight-hour romance, and I was convinced I had met my husband. Side note: twenty-year-old Morgan had a lot left to learn before she was close to dating anyone who was actually husband material!

After those forty-eight hours, my love fantasy quickly turned into a nightmare when Ricardo didn't return my calls. At that time, I didn't even have a cell phone. I had to make phone calls using a barely functional public payphone, and it was the rainy season. There I was, scraping up quarters to go stand in a dirty booth in the rain, only to have my call go straight to voicemail. Womp, womp. It didn't help that there was a language barrier; at that time, my Spanish was mediocre at best. I prayed Ricardo would be able to understand me as I stood there holding the Spanish dictionary in my hands, doing my best to not sound too desperate as I left voicemail after voicemail. News flash: I sounded *very* desperate. I wasn't eating, sleeping, or functioning in any capacity. All I could think of was getting in contact with Ricardo.

Two weeks later in my sleep-deprived, love-disillusioned state, I saw a man who looked like Ricardo driving a Pepsi truck down the street. Naturally, I sprinted after him. After working up quite a sweat, by some miracle, I caught the truck at one of its stops. Of course, the man who got out wasn't, in fact, Ricardo. That's when I hit my knees and shook my fists up at the sky, asking "Whhhhyyyyy???" Why was I acting so crazy, and why on earth was I wasting my valuable energy on a man who wouldn't call me back? I knew the craziness had a root cause, and I knew it needed to stop. I was exhausted. Yes, from the running, but more from the mental and emotional toll that this "love affair" had taken on me. Perhaps you've already guessed that this particular love affair ended with the discovery that Ricardo was married, had three kids, and while he claimed he wanted to leave his family to run away with me, he just couldn't quite pull the trigger. Side note: when you believe that love is unavailable to you, it's amazing the number of married men you will attract!

This Pepsi delivery truck story is just one of many that illustrate my past experiences in love. It wasn't until a decade later that I finally stepped off the dating roller coaster and into a securely attached, confident, and empowered version of myself. The dating roller coaster was painful and nauseating. But here's the thing about pain: it can either motivate you or keep you stuck.

You always have two options when presented with pain:

- Option 1: I can feel this
- Option 2: I can numb this

When you choose door number two, the numbing path, you maintain the pain, and you create what we call suffering. Your existence continues as normal, and nothing changes. You're in what we call "a rut." You're commuting to work, eating dinner each night, and watching Netflix, but you don't really feel present. The pain continues to pile on top of itself, and it grows…so you numb more and more to keep it buried. The problem is that when you numb pain, you also numb joy, happiness, and love. You cut yourself off from *all* emotions. Ultimately this path can be a destructive or emotionally unhealthy route if not course corrected.

If you are one of the few to brave the feeling path, first you feel the pain. Then you process it and learn from it. You incorporate your new learning into your brain's blueprint about the world. Door number one leads to a whole different existence. Feeling the pain is evolution. This path is where the growth and the change is. It is your path to rewiring your brain for a beautiful new reality—one that actually serves and supports you.

I promise to take you down the feeling and healing path in this book. I promise to help you grow—because I couldn't sleep at night if I didn't, and this would instead be a book about the best wines, cheeses, online boutiques, and binge-worthy shows on Netflix. While that may sound like a delightful read, my mission is to serve you and help you get somewhere meaningful in your relationship with yourself and in your romantic relationships.

Getting out of the comfort zone quicksand? It is nearly impossible to do on your own. It's freaking quicksand...haven't you ever seen *The Princess Bride*? That stuff is vicious. It will pull you in for sure. I, for one, could not escape the comfort zone quicksand on my own. That is why I've invested over and over again in books, therapy, coaching, events, and more books. Seriously, you should see my Amazon order history...books on books on books...pretty soon I will need my very own personal library. It is getting way out of hand.

The point is: you're human. Your brain has created its current belief system based on decades of data gathering and experiences, and quite frankly, it has *zero interest* in changing what it knows to be true. This is precisely why we need help when it comes to rewiring our brains. We need therapists, coaches, books, and experts. Think of it this way: you can't see the back of your neck, just like you can't see your unconscious belief systems that are seriously sabotaging you. You need to be both challenged and supported to get out of the comfort zone quicksand. Obviously, you will have to work—I'm not dragging you out of the quicksand, but you best believe I'm tossing you a damn good rope.

I wrote this book for any woman who needs some help finding the love she deserves. This book is exactly what my younger self would have needed to stop the dating madness and finally attract a healthy relationship. You see, building a great relationship did not come easily to me. I watched most of my friends get married while I sat on the sidelines questioning my worthiness and believing something was wrong with me. My early twenties were filled with loneliness, self-loathing, and constantly comparing myself to other people. Emotional highs and lows, and crippling fear of abandonment. At age twenty-five, while completing my second year of graduate school, I began a relationship with a narcissist. For the first six months of our relationship, I did not know he was a narcissist, of course. It started with fun weekends away, fancy dinners out, thoughtful gifts, and a tidal wave of love and adoration. I now know that I was experiencing what is called *love bombing*, the first stage of a relationship with a narcissist. Six months in, our relationship completely shifted from pleasure to immense pain. The person I had believed was my soulmate became my worst nightmare. After six months of experiencing emotional abuse, my self-worth plummeted to its lowest point; I felt like a zombie. I completely hit rock bottom one morning in the lobby of my apartment while filing a police report for the previous night's incident with my toxic boyfriend. I crumbled to my knees in emotional turmoil as the officer said, "I'm so sorry this is happening to you."

From that moment forward, I knew something had to change. I knew I could not keep living that way. It had become a matter of life and death. In the aftermath of the relationship, I decided to slowly put myself back together, and this time, I would only allow healthy relationships into my life. I threw myself into weekly therapy, and I shifted the focus of my graduate studies to revolve around understanding relationship dynamics and attachment theory. I took time away from dating for the first time in my life, and I slowly began to find myself. I started my healing journey. What I didn't realize at the time was that I was paving the way for my dream career.

In 2017, I graduated from Pacific University with a doctorate in clinical psychology, and I devoted my career to helping women heal their pasts and attract great relationships. I became a licensed psychologist in San Diego, California, where I spent two years working at a local university as a psychologist, and then I joined a private practice in La Jolla. I began educating my clients in attachment theory, relationship dynamics, repetition compulsion, and dialogue. I noticed how impactful this information was, and I loved witnessing the joy in people as they began healthy relationships for the very first time in their lives. After two years in private practice, I realized that I had a desire to make a bigger impact. I wanted to help as many women as possible heal and learn how to effortlessly attract a great relationship. I knew that there were so many women out there who needed a framework for healing and a clear path forward.

With this realization, I launched Dr. Morgan Coaching, and I created my signature healing framework, the Empowered Secure Loved method. This framework is a combination of everything I know about healing, cognitive behavioral therapy, neurolinguistic programming, and attachment theory. Beginning a career in coaching enabled me to help people in the way I knew they needed to be helped. While traditional counseling and therapy provide a great space for awareness, coaching enabled me to be direct with clients about what to *do* with the awareness. At this point in time, I am honored to say that the Empowered Secure Loved (E.S.L.) coaching program has helped hundreds of women heal their relationship with themselves and learn how to easily attract a great relationship. Through this work, I have witnessed breakthroughs, complete transformations, weddings, engagements, and women stepping into the highest and best version of themselves. I am grateful every day for the work I get to do and the lives this program has transformed. I feel at peace knowing that I am connected to my highest purpose, and I am doing my part to help end intergenerational cycles of trauma. I love what I do so much that I don't really consider it work. It's simply part of what I'm put on this planet to do. And after coaching hundreds of women inside of the E.S.L. program, I knew it was time to write a book. I knew people needed access to the healing happening inside of the E.S.L. program.

The blood, sweat, and tears that went into birthing this manuscript were all worth it, with the understanding that this book might help even one woman raise her self-worth and get off the dating roller coaster. I wrote this book amidst a global pandemic, the loss of one of my closest friends, and a cross-country move. This book was my refuge in a way, a place I could throw myself into that allowed me to step into my personal zone of genius and feel some hope knowing that these words would help people.

In this book, I will assist you in healing the relationship with yourself, moving toward a secure attachment style, and learning to embody the confident love-magnet version of you. This book is for anyone who has struggled with romantic relationships. If you've ever asked yourself, "What is wrong with me, and why is dating so hard?" this book is for you. Of all the relationships we have in life, a romantic life partner is your most important decision. So what do you do when "finding the one" feels hopeless? How do you change your story when you feel like you're running out of time to truly build the life you want with the love of your life? You start by changing your relationship with yourself and your relationship blueprint. It all starts with your beliefs.

Are you ready for this? Are you ready to examine your past and open the box in your brain labeled DANGER? I hope so. Because This. Is. Your. Life. You deserve to be the creator, the producer, the director, and the leading lady of your own damn life. When you are letting old beliefs run the show, you are giving away your power. You are letting your trauma of the past or your fear for the future steal your joy in the present moment. And guess what! I'm not okay with that. I believe all of us deserve to live lives filled with joy, and we deserve to have belief systems that support us, not sabotage us.

Let's get started by examining those beliefs I just mentioned.

PART ONE

DO THE INTERNAL WORK

CHAPTER ONE

———

BELIEFS ABOUT YOURSELF: MAKE THE UNCONSCIOUS CONSCIOUS

My past client, Amanda, had a history of difficult relationships, always dating guys who wouldn't commit. She came to me in her late twenties, exhausted and ready to find her "forever man." In sorting through her childhood, we realized she had learned she wasn't worthy of love and attention because she "wasn't smart enough." Of course, we processed that this belief was a big, steaming pile of crap and helped her take on a new belief: "I am worthy of love, and healthy romantic love comes to me easily."

Then, within two weeks, she met Mark. Mark was very different from the guys she had dated before. He was "genuinely interested" in her, and they "actually had good conversations!" Amanda was shocked that a guy like him existed. She felt so good and "secure" with Mark. She couldn't believe it. So, what changed? Her belief about herself changed, which allowed her to finally see and *be attracted* to a whole different kind of man. You see, the thing is, guys like Mark are not "unicorns." What gets in the way of letting you see them and *be attracted* to them are your belief system and attachment patterns. Lucky for you, in the pages of this book, we will work on both.

When your beliefs about your worthiness are blocking love, you will see a nice, emotionally available man and go, "Ewwwww! He's weird." Why? Because a man like that does not match up with your beliefs about love. And remember, our brain thrives when our environments match our internal working models of the world. So, when you go around with the belief that you are "never going to find a good man, all the good ones are gone, and dating is so hard," what happens? Your brain seeks out all the scenarios in your environment to confirm those beliefs. Are you ready to drop your limiting, love-blocking, fun-sabotaging beliefs and step into the version of you that is a love magnet? Well, I'm glad you're here. At the end of this chapter, I'm going to walk you through one of the most powerful exercises I teach in the Empowered Secure Loved (E.S.L.) program. It is called "Is This Serving You?"

HUMANITY'S UNIQUE ABILITY

Do you realize as humans we are able to "think about our think-ing?" If you stop to actually ponder this for a second, you'll realize what an absolute *miracle* it is. In this book, I will guide you to examine your current thinking with curiosity and compassion. We will carefully examine your current beliefs about yourself and about relationships. I will challenge you to let go of what is no longer serving you and embrace new beliefs designed to help you step into the best-most-in-love-and-on-fire version of you. The version of you who knows her worth, honors her boundaries, and effortlessly attracts a great relationship. The version of you that you deserve to be, the version of you that the world needs.

The beliefs you developed in childhood were designed to help you survive, not thrive. Think about it this way: If you broke your arm, you'd wear a cast, right? You needed the cast. Your arm was broken! But let's say after your arm healed, you decided to keep wearing the cast—maybe you liked the neon pink color you chose, how you got more attention with a cast, and well, damn, everyone signed their names...so you decided to keep the cast on. Guess what! Keeping a cast on a fully healed arm doesn't help you one tiny bit and just gets in the way of you living your life.

Holding on to the beliefs we develop in childhood due to trauma, loss, neglect, etc., is exactly like continuing to wear a cast when you no longer need one. *At one point* those beliefs served you. They were what you needed *at the time* for survival and daily functioning, but now they are just clunky and raining on your love parade. They are getting in the way of you living your most fulfilled, content, and satisfying life. The crazy part? You might not even realize they are there.

Because as you know, a cast is easy to spot. But unhelpful beliefs built by trauma and pain? Those are sneaky little things. And they are painful as hell to examine. Our brain does all that it can to avoid pain; hence, the brain will do all it can to avoid examining our rigid, old, worn-out beliefs. The brain gets a glimpse of something painful and says, "Danger, danger! Don't go there. It looks like pain lies ahead! Quick! Grab the Oreos, turn on Netflix, drink more merlot, and do some online shopping!" The brain is a master at distraction and avoidance. It knows just how to get you to avoid and to numb. It knows all your favorite ways to stay comfortable, and it loves to suggest them to you. You know what else gets in the way of examining our beliefs? Our brain's insatiable desire to be *right*.

Every human loves to hear "You were right!" And guess what: your brain is no different. Think about it. You gave advice to a friend, and they didn't listen but then came to you later and said, "Geeeez, Heather, you were so right. I should have listened to you! You're so wise." You felt an immediate dopamine release. I-told-you-so energy flooded your veins, and you couldn't help but feel *good*. Your brain is your guidance system. It constructs your realities about the world around you. And more than anything, your brain loves to be *right* because 1) then it doesn't have to work as hard, and 2) it doesn't have to learn anything new. Our brains *love* when the outside world matches our belief system that's been carefully crafted through decades of experience and data collection. When our brains are *right*, they get to be lazy and happy. And since brains are built for survival, they are all about being efficient (a.k.a. lazy). Having to form new pathways and new beliefs about the world? Your brain says, "Eh, I think I'm gonna sit this one out and take a nap instead."

The final thing that gets in the way is your brain's *love* of comfort. Let me make this crystal clear: *our brains are wired for survival*. Not joy, not love, not growth, and most certainly not living your most powerful life, but plain, old, boring survival. Survival—the vanilla flavor of all the emotions, a big yawn of an existence, and you living in scarcity and fear. And guess what. A lot of people go about life in survival mode. A lot of people never question their beliefs, never get out of their own way, and end up feeling comfortable but numb, safe but alone, or peaceful but bored to tears. Maybe you know these types of people. Maybe you are one of these people.

Your comfort zone and the happiest-most-in-love-deeply-fulfilled version of you? They go together like black pants and brown shoes, a bad spray tan and a beach date, a high-heeled stiletto and a grass lawn…you get the idea. Your comfort zone is like quicksand that sucks you away from the sweet destination of growth and happiness. The problem is your brain *likes* to hang out in your comfort zone. If your brain were a person, it would *always* opt for sweatpants, nights in, and the predictable Chinese takeout you've had for the hundredth time. But guess what? *You get to think about your thinking.* Remember the miracle from the beginning of this chapter? You have the opportunity to rewire your brain and change your beliefs. You can tell your brain to get off the couch, throw on a hot outfit, and prepare for success. You are stronger than the comfort zone quicksand.

How do I know? Because I've been there. I hung out in survival mode for years. I stuck to what I knew, and I didn't question it. My environment always matched up to my beliefs, and my views of the world were fairly cemented. The funny thing is that for many of us, our comfort zones are painful if we stop to actually feel into them. When you put down the Cheetos for two seconds, or try to sit and meditate, you realize *whoa, I am actually miserable.* Just because your life is predictable, that doesn't mean you enjoy it. In the past when I was dating the same type of person over and over, I always knew how it would end before it started. It was a predictable roller coaster that landed in a dumpster fire every time. Did it feel good? Hell no! But it was predictable. I knew what would happen. My unconscious knew what would happen, and my brain accepted all the events as "normal." My reality matched what my brain knew to be true about love, my beliefs were confirmed every time, and zero changes in my belief system occurred. To begin to examine your beliefs, we are going all the way back to the beginning, to your childhood.

CHILDHOOD BELIEFS

"So, tell me about your childhood." Has anyone ever said this to you? Surely they have. And let me guess. You didn't launch into a PowerPoint presentation about the episodes of relational trauma you have experienced. "And let's see, here at age seven is when Uncle Mark told me I really should stop eating cookies because my thighs looked like tree trunks. Oh, and how could I forget? Age three, when Mom and Dad got into a fight so bad that Mom drove away in the middle of night, only to return four days later after a tequila-filled bender and an affair. And ah, age seventeen, when Jimmy told me he loved me, but then I learned the next day he had told Alice the exact same thing just two hours after he told me…" The point is, most of us have never taken time to examine the traumatic events of our childhood. And even more uncommon are the people who have taken time to connect the dots between their childhood and their current belief systems.

As a child, you take on the belief systems your parents have given you for *survival*. Your behaviors and belief systems adapt to fit your environment. The truth is, you have no other choice. You can't say at age six, "I think we really ought to use good communication when conflict arises. I'm tired of people breaking dishes and storming off whenever there is an argument in this household!" You are at the mercy of the beliefs and behaviors of your parents, who were at the mercy of the beliefs and behaviors of their parents. Here's what we know: there is a lot of unhelpful shit that gets passed down from generation to generation. Let me remind you, there is hope! Once again, remember the miracle: you get to think about your thinking. You get to turn off "autopilot" and drive the car. Remember, you are the leading lady of your own life. You get to stop playing a supporting role. If the beliefs you learned in childhood are not serving you, guess what! You get to release them, burn them in a bonfire in your backyard, and welcome in a whole new belief system.

Let's get down to business, shall we? The beliefs you have about yourself are usually always connected to a *core belief*. For example, I may have the belief that *I'm too fat for anyone to love me*. The real core belief, buried below this one, however, is *I'm not worthy of love*. As long as you don't deal with the core belief, it will continue to manifest in your life in sneaky ways. Beliefs are typically formed in childhood through either a particularly traumatic experience or through repeated exposure to a way of thinking or behavior.

Let's say you have the belief *I earn love through my accomplishments*. This may have developed because as a child, the only time your parents praised you or gave you attention of any kind was when you won the spelling bee, had a great soccer match, or graduated with honors. In the environment you grew up in, accomplishments meant you'd receive love. And best believe that as humans, knowing we are loved is at the core of our own survival. We will do just about anything to know we are loved. Let's say you carry this belief that accomplishment equals worthiness of love into your dating life as an adult. You may find yourself wanting to tell your partner how you've climbed the ranks in your company this year, placed second in a local 5k race, and won the annual neighborhood chili cook-off. Of course, there is nothing wrong with sharing your accomplishments. However, this may get in the way of a healthy dating relationship if that strategy doesn't get you the desired outcome. What if your partner says=, "Oh, good for you!" and goes on about his day? The response you got from your parents is not happening, and all of a sudden you're sweating, and your brain goes, "Wait a minute! That was supposed to get us love!" Not to mention, when we place conditions on our worthiness of love, it creates anxiety, stress, and pain. What happens when you place fifteenth in the 5k instead of second? You don't feel worthy of love. When love is conditional upon performance, looks, behaviors, etc., love comes and goes. Your self-worth and self-perception of value becomes a roller coaster that sabotages every part of your life imaginable (including your relationships).

Remember what I said about the brain always wanting to be right? This really shows up when we have a belief that love is conditional and then someone tries to give us love. If you don't feel worthy of love because you think you're not successful enough, pretty enough, smart enough, or skinny enough, then even if love showed up on your doorstep with roses and a box of chocolates, you'd tell it to go take a hike. We cannot receive something we do not feel worthy of. If we feel unworthy of an emotionally available, loving, and supportive partner, we will either be blind to those kinds of potential partners, or *if* we do happen to date them, we will find a way to sabotage the relationship. Now, I'm going to guide you through an exercise that will allow you to identify which beliefs are serving you and which beliefs are sabotaging you. I am so excited for you to take this powerful step!

EXERCISE #1: IS THIS SERVING YOU?

First things first, I need you to get out a pen and a journal. Ideally you will use the same journal for all the exercises in this book so you can come back to them as needed. Girl, did you think I was going to let you read this book without doing any actual work? Hell no. Not on my watch. I care about you, which means I need you to be willing to play full-out. Go grab a pen and a journal right now. Make sure you have turned off all distractions in your environment: notifications off; IG/Facebook/Twitter/TikTok can wait! We need your full focus here, right now, on this exercise. You deserve to give that gift to yourself. Please keep in mind you may need some self-care after this exercise, and I encourage you to make time for *yourself* after completing it. Get ready to give yourself the gift of awareness. The new version of you is waiting for you, and she is absolutely amazing.

STEP ONE

For ten minutes, I want you to freewrite, reflecting on the negative/limiting beliefs you have about yourself. Set a timer and let yourself go completely. Close your eyes for a moment before you start, and allow yourself to really drop into your unconscious mind. Allow your mind to wander, and whatever comes up, put it down on the page. Write the following sentence at the top of the page: "The limiting/negative beliefs I have about myself are…" Then go!

STEP TWO

Take a moment to breathe. Inhale. Exhale. Now I want you to identify three core beliefs that lie below the beliefs you just identified. Some common core beliefs include *I am not good enough, I am not worthy of love, I am a failure, I am deeply flawed, I am unlovable, I will always be abandoned…*

STEP THREE

Write the three core beliefs on a new page. Notice how it feels to read them. It should feel kind of uncomfortable. You may have a pain in your chest or feel sick to your stomach.

STEP FOUR

Experiential exercise. I invite you to get really comfortable, and make sure you are breathing deeply into your stomach. You may need to read through these instructions a few times before closing your eyes and completing the exercise.

First, I want you to repeat the three negative core beliefs out loud. Notice how you feel.

Now, reflect on how these beliefs have impacted you in the past. Notice the pain, notice the way they have gotten in the way of what you wanted, and identify how they have impacted you in the *past*. Allow yourself to actually feel the pain these beliefs have caused you.

Next, feel into how these beliefs are impacting you in the *present*. How are they impacting you emotionally? What are they getting in the way of?

Now, go *five years into the future*. What does your life look like if you have clung to your current limiting beliefs? What is the pain like? What is missing in your life? How do you feel, what do you look like, and what is your energy like?

Now I invite you to go *ten years into the future*. What do you feel, holding on to the same limiting, false beliefs about yourself? What is the pain like? What regrets do you have ten years from now?

Finally, I'd like you to go *twenty years into the future*. Imagine twenty years lugging around the limiting beliefs you currently have. How do you feel, what is the pain like, and what does your life look like? Allow yourself to really feel the pain.

STEP FIVE

Place your hand over your heart and say, "I release my old beliefs. My past does not determine my future. Today I choose beliefs that will serve me."

STEP SIX

Write out three empowering beliefs to replace your limiting ones. These should give you a sense of relief, goosebumps, and a feeling of hope. You may have to play with them a bit. Examples include the following:

I am worthy of love.

Love flows to me easily.

I am unstoppable and deserving of success.

I am beautiful inside and out.

I am deserving of all my heart's desires.

Note about this exercise: You can keep going into the future until you hit your deathbed, if that's your thing, and if you feel the pain will help you let go of beliefs. Also, this *should cause pain.* Remember, pain is a motivator. The pain you feel today while doing this exercise is a gift to your future self. Allow yourself to feel it, then decide to use it for good.

Now that you have let go of the beliefs about yourself that are holding you back, let's learn exactly how to rewire your brain to enable you to attract healthy relationships.

CHAPTER TWO

BELIEFS ABOUT RELATIONSHIPS

REWIRE YOUR BRAIN TO SUPPORT A GREAT RELATIONSHIP

In my early twenties, I dated some real characters. There was a really fascinating one; let's call him John. John liked to drink wine. A lot. He was a writer, and perhaps he thought he was the next Hunter S. Thompson. A red flag was when he told me he needed his "driving wine" and proceeded to fill a thermos with merlot as we hopped into his almost-always-broken-down Subaru. And I will never forget another particularly bright red flag. He had gotten his house key stuck in his front doorknob, and instead of repairing it, he carried his doorknob around everywhere we went. I laughed about it at the time (y'all, he literally had a doorknob in his hand at all times), but the reality was incredibly sad. I was chasing an alcoholic with no emotional availability, a huge drinking problem, and no capacity whatsoever for a real relationship. And of course, this kind of relationship dynamic fit very nicely with my core relationship beliefs at the time, that love was not available to me, and that I must work very hard for love.

In this chapter, I am going to help you examine your beliefs about relationships and go through some of the foundational steps for creating a brand-new "blank love slate," aka not carrying over your past relationship experiences into your present and future ones.

AVOIDING THE BURN OF LOVE

Does your brain think love is a hot stove? What exactly happens when the brain associates something with pain? It avoids it at all costs. If your brain has associated intimacy, closeness, dating, or relationships with pain, then it wants to keep you the hell away from it. Consciously, you may say, "I am ready for Mr. Right, a house, three babies, and the soccer-mom van. Bring it on!" But unconsciously, your brain is saying, "No way, José. I won't let you get hurt again. Remember the last time we tried that? You wouldn't get out of bed for three weeks, watched *The Notebook* fifty-seven times, and ate your weight in Dove chocolate. We are not going there again, amigo. A person can only handle so much Nicholas Sparks!" This is often why people take two steps toward love and then three steps back. Their brain sends out the message of "Alert! Alert! Intimacy is near! Must exit immediately or do something stupid to mess this up!"

Let's take this a step further. Do you remember the baby Albert study from Psychology 101? Poor Albert. A psychologist named John Watson would hit a metal pipe with a hammer every time nine-month-old Albert was exposed to a white rat. What happened? Albert became terrified of the white rat! (Geez, psychologists have done some crazy experiments. Looking at you, Stanford prison experiment! But that's a story for another time.) What was fascinating to experimenters in the baby Albert study was that Albert developed a phobia of *all* things white and fuzzy. Cute, friendly, white bunny rabbit? Albert was terrified. White fur coat? Albert was inconsolable. Santa's white beard? Albert screamed in agony. Through this research, psychologists discovered something we call "stimulus generalization," the over-generalization of a fear response toward objects that appear similar to the stimuli that provoked a fear response. In other words, we tend to jump to conclusions about new stimuli that are similar to past stimuli that caused us pain. It is the way our brains are designed! Poor Albert never recovered from his phobia, by the way. The good news is that you're here, reading this book, so unlike Albert, you will have the tools to help you leave the past in the past.

Let's apply stimulus generalization to relationships, shall we? Let's say your emotionally abusive, unfaithful loser ex-boyfriend was really into watching scary movies. He loved *Saw* (parts one through six), *The Ring*, and especially Alfred Hitchcock movies. Fast-forward to three years later. You're on a date that seems to be going well, *until* sweet Gerardo mentions that he loves horror films! Especially Hitchcock. Your brain goes, "Ooooooh, shit. Another one of *those!*" Your brain has overgeneralized that anyone who likes horror films is a poor choice for a partner. The same goes for becoming closer to someone. When your brain has associated intimacy with pain, it will urge you to "run" at the first sign of intimacy.

In the same way that you develop beliefs about yourself, you develop beliefs about relationships. These beliefs are developed from your experiences. Here are some common unhelpful beliefs:

1. Relationships never work out for me.
2. I need to achieve or be productive in order to earn love.

3. Everyone I date will leave me/cheat on me/hurt me badly.
4. I will always be abandoned.
5. My needs don't matter; I should focus on pleasing my partner.
6. There are no good men out there.
7. Love is unavailable to me; I will never feel adored/desired.
8. I am not good enough for the kind of man I want to date.
9. I am not pretty enough for a good relationship.
10. I can't be successful in my career *and* have a great relationship.
11. I won't be physically attracted to a secure, healthy partner.
12. There is something wrong with me that will always sabotage my relationships.

LAUNCHING YOUR LIMITING BELIEFS: MELINDA AND SAMANTHA'S STORIES

These beliefs about relationships impact how we make decisions about dating. And they tend to do it in a sneaky way. Take my client Melinda for example. Before completing the E.S.L. relationship program, she always found herself in long-distance relationships with partners who were ultimately unfaithful to her. She could not figure it out. It turns out she was carrying a model from past relationships: love is unavailable, intimacy is scary, and if I'm close with someone, they will leave me. The partners Melinda chose again and again were not available to her. The reality? She didn't feel *safe* dating someone who actually had the capacity for emotional intimacy. So her brain came up with a solution: in order to have a relationship and "stay safe," she would date guys with different area codes who were not actually interested in a long-term partnership. This may have seemed like a creative solution, but ultimately, it wasn't effective at all, and it was based on limiting beliefs and past trauma. Melinda's story is a perfect example of how our brains can prioritize safety over our happiness in relationships.

Once Melinda identified her core relationship beliefs and was able to let go of the root relational trauma responsible for these relationship patterns, she was finally able to date an entirely new kind of partner. She was able to meet a *local* guy (funny enough, he lived a couple blocks from her), and they proceeded to get engaged and later married. All because Melinda was willing to examine her dating patterns and rewire her beliefs about relationships.

My client Samantha had a history of unconsciously selecting emotionally (and sometimes even physically) abusive partners. Her relationship blueprint was doomed from the start with her father being a complete jerk to her mom. Early on in life, she witnessed her dad perpetrating abuse toward her mom. What was even more confusing is that she also witnessed them having very tender moments of closeness and intimacy. Her relationship blueprint indicated that with intimacy comes pain, and to be close to someone is to experience abuse. I want to make one thing clear: emotional and physical abuse is NEVER the receiver's fault. Just because you unconsciously feel drawn to painful relationships, the abuse is never, ever, *ever* your fault. In our work together, Samantha learned she had associated love with chaos. We worked together to create a new relationship blueprint for her, where love became safe, stable, and supportive. She almost immediately began dating a whole different kind of partner with whom she continues to grow. She changed her blueprint, and secure love followed effortlessly.

Let's apply this to you, shall we? Buckle up because we're about to get vulnerable. Don't worry. I've got you, and you've got this next exercise! In order to help you understand your patterns and beliefs, I'll take you through an exercise I call the "Relationship

Inventory." We will examine your past significant relationships so that you can gain insight into your current patterns and beliefs. This exercise is guaranteed to rock your relationship world and make way for a whole new securely attached foundation.

But before we get started, imagine you want to buy a nice couch. Real adulting here, people. I'm not talking IKEA; I mean a *nice* couch, potentially something from West Elm or a chestnut leather statement piece. Maybe in the past you only had hand-me-down or garage-sale discount couches. And that was fine because that was what was affordable and available. The old, horribly outdated, dirty, can't-bear-to-look-at-it (possibly red plaid or brown/orange flower print) couch still sits in your living room. Here's the deal: you won't be able to welcome in your dream couch until the old one is gone. And here's the real kicker: as long as the couch is still in your living room, you will be tempted to settle for it. You'll say, "It's not that bad, *really*...I mean, sure, every time my friends visit, I throw a blanket over the hideous floral pattern, buuuut it's just *such* a comfy couch. Maybe it will be fine for a while longer?" Your old relationship patterns are like that couch. They are taking up valuable space in your brain and preventing you from upgrading! It's time to get rid of your old relationship model and bring in the new. You deserve to upgrade. And guess what! In order to bring in the new relationship model, we do have to fully get rid of the old. You wouldn't try to stack two couches on top of each other in your living room, right? I'd hope not! In the same way, you don't want your old relationship model to get in the way of your new one. It's time to kick it to the curb—tell it to hit the road and find someone who still likes floral patterns. It is time to make room for your new relationship model. Let's do this.

EXERCISE #2: RELATIONSHIP INVENTORY

For this exercise, make sure you have your journal handy. You will likely come back to this exercise many times. I want you to identify the significant relationships in your past. By significant, I mean relationships that have had an impact on you. This begins with your parents or childhood caregivers and likely ends with your last romantic relationship.

Write each name out on the top of a page, and leave a whole page for each person. I want you to take some deep breaths in now and say these words to yourself: "I will not judge any thoughts that arise. I am committed to understanding my past and sending myself compassion. I can do this, and I will. I am worthy of healing."

For each person you identified, I want you to freewrite and answer the following questions:

1. Did I feel safe in this relationship (emotionally, physically, etc.)?
2. Did I feel heard and understood?
3. Were my needs met?
4. Could I express my needs and set boundaries?
5. Did I feel loved/appreciated? If not, why?

Note about how to complete this exercise well:

Take deep breaths. Know that nothing worthwhile is ever easy. Allow yourself to write whatever comes to mind, releasing all judgment. Send the younger version of yourself so much compassion and love.

This inventory exercise accomplishes a couple of things. Number one, it opens you up to understanding your past patterns. This is incredibly important because without understanding, we do not have acceptance, and without acceptance, we do not have change. Some of you may realize that the patterns you are repeating started from your relationship with a sibling or from your very first love interest. We owe it to ourselves to be curious about the origin of our patterns. Number two, the inventory allows you to have compassion for the younger version of you. It encourages you to acknowledge the ways you have been "failed." All relationships have failures—we have all been let down before. No matter how incredible your parents were, all of us have experienced relational dysfunction in our lives at some point. So, it is important to remember the following phrase when realizing there were failures from the people close to us: "My caregivers did the best they could, and there are ways that they failed me." Both parts of this statement are true.

A very important note about moving forward: it does not matter how dysfunctional your past was. There is no "too damaged" disclaimer for your future. Even if all your past relationships have ended in dumpster fires, affairs, or restraining orders, you can wipe your relationship slate completely clean. I personally thought I was "beyond repair." There was a time I believed I was simply "too damaged" to ever have a great relationship. I did not believe it was available to me. Once I got out of my own way and accepted that healing was in fact possible, I was able to let go of my past and open a completely new chapter in my dating life. You deserve to do the same. No matter how painful this exercise is, please know it is a *huge* step in the right direction. Give yourself a high five in the mirror, a pat on the back, or a nice hug. You are on your way to healing! Next, let's accelerate that healing by diving into self-care as the best maintenance for being your best self.

CHAPTER THREE

FERRARI MAINTENANCE

Hey, girl, I have an important announcement for you. You're not a Prius. You're a damn Ferrari. What on earth do I mean when I say this? I mean you deserve to be *high maintenance*. When I say "high maintenance," I'm not talking about a Starbucks order that is three pages long and a set of two-inch acrylic nails. High maintenance means you know that in order to function as your best self, you need a high level of self-care. You need high levels of energy investment into yourself. Think about this: when you take good care of yourself, everything in life is easier. I have a favorite quote I write on my bathroom mirror: "When I feel good, life feels easy." When you are aware of what it takes to perform at a high level/feel your best/love at your best *and* you make time for those things in your life? Well, my dear, that is the key to unlocking your best self and ultimately welcoming a great relationship.

Before we go further, I need to clarify that "self-care" in the way I refer to it means any time you tune in to yourself, ask yourself what you need, and honor whatever comes up. It is not about mani-pedis or bubble baths. (Although, if you tune in and a bubble bath *is* what you need, then yes, that is self-care!) True self-care is about asking yourself, "What habits, boundaries, and methods of communication do I need in order to be the version of me that kicks ass, takes names, and feels at peace?" The version of me who stands in her truth, has fulfilling relationships, and does not feel "tired all the time." The version of me who can laugh out loud, can dance unapologetically, and knows how to have a good time. The version of me who isn't afraid to show up in the world with a smile and an energy that says, "I know what I want, Universe. Please deliver it to me. Thank you in advance." Girl, that version of you exists right now, and she requires Ferrari maintenance.

Many of us haven't gone through life with rock-solid levels of self-worth. Most of us need major self-worth repair and rebuilding. If your self-worth is a house, it needs much more than a new coat of paint. We need to strip away the things that aren't working, keep only the good bones, and build from there. The truth is that your lack of self-worth is causing your poor habits, and your poor habits are *maintaining* your low self-worth. Read that again. This is a vicious cycle that must be stopped if you want real, lasting transformation that catapults you into the life you desire and the kind of relationships you deserve.

ACTIONS BECOME HABITS

One of the most effective ways to rebuild your self-worth is through your daily actions. When your behaviors become the behaviors of someone who loves herself unapologetically and prioritizes her needs, your self-worth responds by healing and becoming stronger. For the majority of us, we cannot think our way into becoming someone who has high levels of self-worth, but we can act our way into a new way of being. This chapter is dedicated to making sure you have all the necessary tools to help you actively rebuild and maintain rock-solid self-worth. Because guess what?! Having high levels of self-worth is the foundation for attracting and maintaining that loving partnership you desire.

Let's talk about the B.S. that gets in the way of Ferrari maintenance. In other words, the lies that prevent you from taking good care of yourself. Many women I work with will say, "I don't have time" or "Other things are more important." Girl. When you don't make time to take care of yourself, you sabotage every area of your life. You show up as the watered-down, worn-out, low-energy version of you, and it prevents you from living the life you truly desire. There is a great metaphor I heard from Rachel Hollis about this. Let's say you have a vase of flowers, where the flowers and vase represent you, and the water is your energy. If you are constantly bending, giving, almost tipping over, and giving your energy to everyone but yourself, eventually, the vase completely empties its water supply, topples over, and shatters into a million pieces. This experience is known as burnout. Trust me. I've been there a few times. It is not pretty, and oftentimes it takes months (or years) to recover. The alternative to you shattering into pieces and having to slowly glue yourself back together is this: fill up your vase with water. Give to yourself first. Stand tall. Don't overextend yourself. Let boundaries guide your giving. Prioritize *yourself* and let the water overflow so that you may give your energy to others from a place of abundance. When we give from abundance, it feels better. And it is more impactful to all involved.

Another lie is that you're not "worthy" of self-care and others need your energy more than you do. This may be an unconscious lie, perhaps originating from parents who were emotionally neglectful, chronically invalidating, or limited in their capacity to be tuned in to your needs. When we are treated from an early age as though our needs don't matter, we internalize this to be true, and we begin to respond to ourselves as though our needs don't matter. In a nutshell, you treat *yourself* how you were treated as a child. I have helped many women uncover the unconscious limiting beliefs that have prevented them from honoring the level of self-care they deserve. These beliefs can be extremely sneaky, and you may need to revisit Exercise #1: Is This Serving You? (from Chapter 1) in order to fully remove the barriers to creating self-care.

Here's the thing: your struggles with self-worth are not your fault. It is likely that you lost the connection with your needs, wants, preferences, and desires because growing up, you learned to stop tuning inward. Either your voice was not heard when you did express your needs, or your voice was heard, and it was invalidated or criticized. When we are children, if we learn that our needs will not be honored, we learn to ignore them so we can maintain a relationship with our caregivers. We do this out of survival. But now you are a grown adult, and it is time to reconnect to your internal experience, aka your internal guidance system.

LET'S. GET. DOWN. TO. BUSINESS.

How do you do something you've never done? You model it after someone who does it successfully. You experiment, keep the things that work, and throw out the rest. You drop judgment and give yourself permission to be curious about what it takes for you to show up as the highest version of you. Essentially, you need to be a *self-love* scientist. On social media and on the *Let's Get Vulnerable* podcast, I talk a lot about being a love scientist when dating, but this also applies to discovering your magic Ferrari maintenance formula.

I will give you a personal example of being a scientist about self-love. In the past, I used to believe that I *needed* to indulge in shopping sprees once or twice a month. You know the kind. Show up at the mall empty-handed, and leave with a minimum of five bags. Use a credit card in the name of "doing something for me." On the surface, this looked like self-love and spoiling myself. However, when I dug deeper, I realized these shopping sprees were usually preceded by a period of feeling down or just "off." I noticed that I'd only feel better for a few hours afterward, and then plummet to feeling even more miserable later. I realized that the things I bought were often impulse buys and would sit in my closet never to be worn. The shopping spree that I labeled as an act of self-love was actually a numbing skill designed to help me block out uncomfortable emotions. Distraction as a coping skill does more harm than good. In your role as a self-care scientist, be on the lookout for distraction disguised as self-care.

Let's take it a bit deeper, shall we? When I was honest about my numbing behavior patterns, I realized it was the exact behavior I saw my mother engage in when I was a young girl. When she was frustrated with my dad or with work, I remember us hopping into her old blue Volvo to go to the mall and buy things. It was either that or eating Oreos by the sleeve. And yes, emotional eating was also something I had to unlearn. I had been repeating the numbing behaviors that were modeled for me as a little girl, and they were not helping me in the slightest. This is what "getting curious" allows us to do. We must let go of the behaviors that maintain low self-worth so that we can fill up our energy cup with behaviors (and thoughts) that truly serve us. I invite you to go look in the mirror and be honest about your current behaviors. Then go answer the golden question in your journal: are these behaviors serving me?

EXERCISE #3.1: SELF-CARE SCIENTIST STARTER PACK (THE HABIT INVENTORY)

As you become a self-care scientist, I want to help you by giving you some questions to ask yourself about your current coping and self-care habits. I want to invite you to take each of your current habits and answer the following questions in your journal:

1. When do I do this? Is it following any specific emotions?
2. Why do I do this? What is the benefit I get from this habit?
3. Is this adding value to my life, or taking my energy?
4. Is this a habit I want to keep, or is there a replacement habit that would serve me better?

Let's walk through an example where I take a closer look at two common self-care habits. This should give you an idea for how to fill out this habit inventory:

HABIT: EXERCISING FIVE TIMES A WEEK

1. I do this in the morning. Sometimes it is following stress, feeling overwhelmed, or feeling tired.
2. I do this to care for my body and to give back to my mind. I feel more energized and well taken care of mentally when I work out.
3. It is adding value to my life.
4. I want to keep this habit and continue to prioritize it.

HABIT: DRINKING ALCOHOL

1. I do this late at night while watching Netflix. I might feel lonely, stressed, tired, or bored.
2. I do this to numb how I am feeling and to distract myself. I

temporarily distract from what I am feeling. I don't have to take ownership of my emotions in the moment.

3. This habit is taking value from my life. It impacts my sleep and keeps me stuck emotionally.
4. I want to replace drinking alcohol with sleeping, drinking tea, or journaling through my emotions.

Once you've gotten rid of what is no longer serving you, it is time to make room for the *good*, baby! This is when the rubber meets the road, the nozzle meets the gas tank, the air goes into the tire (I'm curious how many car metaphors I can get into one sentence, but I will spare you from any additional ones).

I have something really important to tell you. You *can* be in charge of your state. I had always known this to be true, but it wasn't until I attended a Tony Robbins *Unleash the Power Within* event in Los Angeles that this truth became crystal clear to me. Here's the deal: the first day at the event, you dance, jump, scream, cry, and run around for about fourteen hours straight. And oh yeah, you walk on hot burning coals at the very end of the night. (Y'all, I did walk on the hot coals, and no, my feet did not get burned! #energyonpoint) I had a freaking blast. I felt like lightning bolts were coursing through my veins. I was unstoppable for fourteen hours straight. And here's what I learned: We can be intentional with our energy. We can decide our mental and emotional state by intentionally choosing our *actions, thoughts,* and *behaviors.* In this event, this fact is taken to the extreme so that you can no longer ignore your own power.

I am not saying that you should sing, jump, and dance your way through your day. However, I do know this: You deserve to be filled with energy. You deserve to feel momentum pulling you forward. You deserve to feel connected to your inner self, the universe, and the vision you have for your life. I have helped hundreds of women cultivate these feelings in their daily lives, and I want to share those secrets with you. But first, I need to ask you something. Are you willing to get uncomfortable? Are you willing to feel silly, weird, or cheesy? Are you willing to play full-out for the life you want? Or do you prefer to stay comfortable and stuck where you are? The choice is up to you. However, I urge you to choose to play full-out so you can get the most out of the secrets I am about to share with you.

MORNING ALIGNMENT

What if I told you that you can intentionally connect to the life you desire? You can intentionally tune in to the frequency that effortlessly attracts what is meant for you. I believe what is meant for you comes to you effortlessly when you tune in and listen to your heart's deepest desires (and honor those desires). So many of us have never made the time to tune inward; most of us are too distracted by the outward noise to make time to go internal.

I want to help you change that. I am going to teach you a powerful practice I call the "Morning Alignment." When women go through the E.S.L program, they learn the exact formula I use for this practice, and they get a sneak peek into my very own personal Morning Alignment ritual. For the purposes of this book, I want to provide you with a starting point. I'll provide a link in the next section.

Why must you do this life-changing ritual in the morning? The thoughts and feelings that you cultivate in the morning set the tone for your *entire* day. I want to make sure you are embodying the energy that sets you up for attracting what you desire. I want to make sure you feel connected to the vision you have for your life and your life's purpose.

The Morning Alignment (MA) is both a ritual and a living, breathing document that you create. Personally, I have created my MA document in a Google doc so that I can make changes to it and access it easily. This ritual should become a *daily* habit that takes about ten to fifteen minutes. That's only ten to fifteen minutes a day to change the trajectory of your life. Is it worth it to you? I sure hope so!

Let's get started!

EXERCISE #3.2: CREATING YOUR MORNING ALIGNMENT DOCUMENT

In the E.S.L. program, I guide my clients to create a detailed document that has *six* different sections designed to help them walk confidently in the direction of their dreams. I want to walk you through three of those sections so you can get started with this highly impactful daily practice. Go to www.drmorgancoaching.com/lovemagnetgifts to download the PDF that goes along with this exercise.

1. VISION MAP

This section is designed for you to paint the full picture of your future. You are to write out the vision for your life. Don't be afraid to ask yourself what you *really, truly* desire. Be honest, be vulnerable, and get it written down! While you can write this down in a journal, I highly recommend visiting the above webpage and creating your own document. Here is an example to get you started:

> Morgan Anderson is a highly successful relationship coach and heart-centered entrepreneur. She is a high-value partner and an incredible daughter. She cares deeply about her clients and is committed to making a positive impact on the world. She loves her family and spends quality time with them as often as she wants. She travels when she wants, gives to charities of her choice, and lives in an energy of abundance and love. She is fulfilled, abundant, and free.

2. AFFIRMATIONS

We've all heard it before, but it is absolutely true: affirmations work. In this section, you are to list affirmations that speak into existence the next-level version of you—the version that is already there within you and simply needs permission to emerge. Another important reminder is that these affirmations need to *speak to you*. When you read them, they should give you goosebumps and pull you forward. Whatever kind of language speaks to you, use that language. Need cuss words? Use cuss words. Need Bible verses? Use those. Use whatever language empowers you and calls out the truth of who you are.

3. THEATER OF THE MIND

Also known as a "vision board," this section is comprised of *images* that speak to you about your future. Images that give you goose-bumps to look at because they speak to the vision you have for your life. I have also included ten core identity I AM statements in this section that help me solidify my identity and what is most important to me.

CREATING YOUR MORNING ALIGNMENT RITUAL PRACTICE

Okay y'all, I have made this a habit because I do it when my eyes open *first thing* in the morning. I practice this ritual as soon as my alarm goes off. It is the first thing I do. I do it before I get out of bed, before I check my phone/email/Slack channel, before I work out, before I drink my coffee. Even before I go to the bathroom, and sometimes before I even sit up in bed. Like I said, *first thing.* And I can say after doing it for years, it has helped me *enjoy* my mornings and start my day with peace and confidence. When you start your day fueling up your gas tank, you show up better, and you come from a place of giving. When you do it consistently, this ritual will become an energizing and life-giving part of your morning routine.

THE PRACTICE

First, I want to invite you to focus on your breathing. Begin by taking deep breaths into your stomach and let go of any tension you feel. Get into a place of complete relaxation and openness. A place of surrender and hope. A place of gratitude and power. Tune in to your internal self and open up your morning alignment document. Here you will read through the document and take in each section. The rest of the day, know that you can pull up this document as needed. At any time, you have access to your future self. At any time in the day, you can reconnect to the frequency of your higher self. What a powerful realization!

I want to give you a high five and a hug right now. You have made it through the first part of this book, and you are well on your way to becoming a confident, securely attached love magnet. These first three chapters were designed to help you take a journey inward and do the foundational healing necessary to welcome a great relationship. In the next part of the book, we are going to shift our focus to understanding attachment theory and your relationship patterns.

PART TWO

ATTACHMENT THEORY

CHAPTER FOUR

SO, WHAT IS ATTACHMENT THEORY ANYWAY?

I stared at my phone. He hadn't texted me yet. It was Valentine's Day, 2015. I stood in the kitchen with all the ingredients to a pasta dish he said he wanted us to make together. I paced the kitchen as I manically typed and then deleted several multiple-paragraph text messages. I felt sick to my stomach. 7:30, 8:00, 9:00, and still nothing. Finally, at around 11:00 p.m., I cried myself to sleep after drinking half of the bottle of wine we were supposed to enjoy together. I imagined all sorts of scenarios. Had Steven gone out with someone else? Or maybe he realized he could do better than me…or did he just get too drunk? As I woke up hungover at 8:00 the next morning, I asked myself, "Why do I keep dating assholes?" Then a text popped up on my phone. It was Steven. I felt as though I might puke. The text read: "Hi. Wyd?" Rage flooded my body as I realized he wasn't even going to acknowledge that he had flaked on our Valentine's dinner. The nerve of this dude! This memory is just one example of the many times dating emotionally unavailable men caused chaos and pain in my life. My disorganized attachment style was ruining my happiness and getting in the way of my dream of having a great relationship.

Spoiler alert: Steven was one of the last avoidantly attached men I ever invested time with. It turned out he was dating multiple women at once, and I was completely on his "relationship backburner." The thing about repeating unhealthy relationship patterns is that no matter how infuriated you are that it is happening, you will continue to do it until you heal. A very important part of getting off of the dating roller coaster is acknowledging toxic dating patterns and understanding *why* you keep doing what you're doing in love. If only there was a framework for understanding relationship functioning. Oh wait! There is. And you need it. I'd like to introduce you to your healthy relationship best friend, attachment theory.

Okay, girl, I'm gonna be honest with you. I am a huge nerd when it comes to attachment theory. I have devoted my career to understanding how you can easily apply it to your dating life and become a healthier, more confident partner. This part of the book is going to be a game changer for you when it comes to finally understanding your dating patterns and learning how to *embody* the securely attached woman. My promise to you is that these upcoming pages will be easy to understand, and I will provide real-world examples that bring these concepts to life. You will get to feel like an attachment theory expert without having to read hundreds of dry research articles. I've got you covered, and I am so excited for you to finally get the missing piece to the dating puzzle: understanding attachment theory!

CONNECTION IS OXYGEN

First off, let's get one thing straight: to connect is to be human. In the same way we need food, shelter, oxygen, and warmth, we *need* to give love and to receive love in return. Attachment theory in its simplest form is understanding relationship patterns and the "why" behind what we do in relationships. Buckle up because in this chapter, we are going to do a deep dive on the science of attachment theory, and you will understand exactly why I call attachment theory "the missing piece of the dating puzzle." Attachment theory will not only help you understand *why* you do what you do, but it will also help you decode:

- why you are attracted to the "type" of person you are attracted to;
- why your partner does what they do in a relationship;
- patterns in your dating life that previously seemed mystifying; and
- what your true needs are in order to feel emotionally safe in a relationship.

From the beginning, we are all wired for connection. Our brains develop in ways that support us in creating relationships with other humans. Of course, in prehistoric times, an added benefit of relationships included not being eaten by a saber-toothed tiger, whereas these days, the benefits include improved emotional, psychological, and physical functioning. In the research studies that gave birth to attachment theory, John Bowlby and Mary Ainsworth discovered the attachment systems of baby monkeys. They discovered that when their mother was taken from them, the baby monkey would choose a terry cloth over any other comfort (even food!) simply because the terry cloth reminded them of their mother. As children, we *need* to feel connected to our caregivers, and then as adults, that need transfers over to our romantic partners who become our source of security, our stable bond, and our predictable source of emotional support.

SECURE BASE

Relationships that provide reassurance, support, and warmth are one of the magic ingredients to a successful life. When we feel secure in our relationships, it frees us up to take risks, show up big in our lives, and "play full-out." A securely attached relationship adds value to your life, provides a safety net below you (should you fall), and supports you in developing your own high levels of self-worth. You deserve to live a life supported by relationships that add value to you, instead of feeling dragged down by relationships that suck your energy and add anxiety to your life. When you have a relationship that feels secure, you are not wasting your energy "trying hard not to be abandoned." You are not consumed by feelings of unworthiness, self-doubt, or fear. Your precious energy is freed up to focus on growing, learning, and becoming the very best version of you! This truth is ultimately why I love the work I do. I know that when I help women have great relationships, I simultaneously help them have great *lives*. A secure base with yourself and a secure base with your romantic partner frees you up to make the impact you want to make in the world. It gives your energy, focus, and power back. It creates a rock-solid foundation for your dream life.

UNDERSTANDING YOUR ATTACHMENT SYSTEM

Let's go back to childhood, shall we? (C'mon, as a psychologist you know I've got to bring up your childhood as many times as possible.) Remember, as a child you *had* to connect with your parents or caregivers for survival. You had to adapt to whatever relationship blueprint they provided for you. It was necessary for your survival that you behaved in ways that secured their love and attention. To think you had any other choice is fooling yourself.

As children, we learn to change our thoughts and behaviors in relationships in order to feel safe and loved. Our brain develops neural pathways that dictate how we respond to experiences in relationships. From the moment you are born, beliefs begin developing about yourself and relationships; those beliefs begin to form your behaviors and "ways of being" in a relationship. Thus, without your conscious awareness, your attachment style begins to form at an early age.

So why does your shit show up in your romantic relationships?

Women I'm coaching often say to me, "I don't understand. All of my friendships and family relationships are great. I feel loved, adored, appreciated, and valued in my friendships. I can set boundaries, express my needs, and feel very healthy in those relationships. So *why on earth* are my romantic relationships so tumultuous?" Here's why: You are most vulnerable in your romantic relationships, and due to dependence on your partner for survival (as ingrained in us from ancient times), this is where your true relationship blueprints show up. Not to mention, any unresolved parental trauma is automatically transferred to the romantic partnership. This is the place your wounded child shows up and the container in which unhealthy relationship patterns show themselves.

MOVING TO SECURE ATTACHMENT: YOU CAN DO IT

Here's the deal: a lot of attachment theory researchers have claimed that your attachment style (aka your unique way of being in relationships) is set in stone. It's kind of like the set point theory when it comes to weight loss. Some researchers argue that your body has a set weight at which it wants to be and will always return to, and that's that. Diet all you want, run, eat chicken and broccoli, but your weight will always return to its "set point." In the same way, some researchers believe that your attachment style is set where it is, and that's that. Through my own research, my own experience, and my clients' experiences, I have gone directly against this belief. The truth is you can always move toward a secure attachment style. Let me say that again: *you can always move toward a secure attachment style.* (Which is where we all want to be, by the way, and I'll say more about what this means later.)

ANXIOUS, AVOIDANT, DISORGANIZED, SECURE... WHICH AM I?

Now it's time to break down each attachment style and get you started on your way to becoming an attachment theory pro! I want you to read through this next section with an open mind. Don't worry; at the end of this chapter, I will hook you up with access to an attachment style quiz that will provide you with insight into your own unique attachment style. For each attachment style, I will provide you with a basic definition, real-life examples, typical thought patterns, and attachment strategies unique to each style. Let's do this!

ATTACHMENT STYLE #1: ANXIOUS ATTACHMENT
Definition

Anxious attachment: I'd rather lose myself than lose a relationship. I have a fear of abandonment and believe I need to be on alert in order to prevent this from happening. I overvalue my partner, and I devalue myself. I often interpret my partner's behaviors as signs of disinterest and future abandonment.

Anxious Attachment Behaviors

- Seeks constant reassurance
- Exhibits protest behaviors: "testing" to see if your partner "really" loves you, ignoring contact, pushing someone away, overcontacting, or large displays of affection
- Has difficulty expressing needs/emotions/wants
- Internalizes relationship failings as "all my fault"
- Daydreams about ex
- Devalues self, highly values partner
- Feels emotionally exhausted when dating
- Gives too much in relationships and has difficulty setting boundaries
- Overvalues closeness and intimacy

Anxious Attachment Thoughts

"What if this doesn't work out?"

"Am I good enough for my partner?"

"Does my partner actually like me?"

"How can I make my partner's life better?"

"What if they cheat on me/leave me/hurt me...?"

"I just want to know they care about me and need me."

"I know my partner doesn't love me as much as I love them."

"I am too much. If I express myself, they will leave."

"I always sabotage everything. Why can't I do anything right?"

"I feel like I'm losing myself in this relationship, but I don't know how to stop it."

Have you ever stared at your phone, waiting for that text back, and started to physically sweat? It's been five minutes and they have not texted you back! Pretty soon, your mind goes down a catastrophizing spiral of impending relationship doom: *What if they don't like me anymore? OMG, they are probably hanging out with someone else…maybe it's that girl from the coffee shop he talked to last weekend! Aaaaah! What if he didn't like that it was me who initiated sex last time? What if he didn't like the shoes I wore? OMG, if this relationship ends, I'll have to listen to Aunt Brenda's "careful or you'll end up a spinster dog lady and die alone" speech…I cannot hear that speech again!*

Ooooof. This kind of thought spiral is exhausting, distracting, and downright ugly. It can make you ignore your friends, ignore your workday, and decide to go back to bed and pull the covers tightly over your head. It can make you want to throw your phone off a bridge and then pull your hair out. If you have found yourself catastrophizing, overthinking, and predicting the death of your relationship, you have suffered from anxious attachment behaviors. To illustrate this, let's examine one of my past client's experiences.

Selena's Story

Selena was tired of being single and felt she kept repeating the same patterns over and over. Each time she went through a breakup, she became more jaded about love and more convinced she'd die alone. She was ready to throw in the towel and never date again. (Thank goodness that deep-down part of her knew that there were things within her control that she could work on.) Before our work together, she had dated a string of emotionally unavailable men. One particularly painful breakup occurred after her fiancé at the time cheated on her and explained that he "wasn't ready for commitment." She was devastated and blamed herself completely.

Selena displayed classic anxious attachment dating beliefs and behaviors. After a thorough assessment, I was confident that anxious attachment strategies dominated her approach to love. Selena explained that she felt exhausted when dating, and she just didn't get why love "never worked out for her" when she had tried *so hard* to make every relationship work. I explained to Selena that she had an overactive anxious attachment system—that her brain was wired to "work hard" in love. I explained that her behaviors were designed to help her feel secure in relationships and that currently she needed high levels of reassurance to be able to "feel safe in love." I communicated to her that while these behaviors were coping strategies designed to get her emotional safety needs met in relationships, they often backfired and contributed to her partners' decision to end a relationship. Her fear of abandonment became a self-fulfilling prophecy when her anxious attachment strategies went unchecked.

I explained that she learned these behaviors through experience with her early caregivers. She had learned she needed to be preoccupied with her security object (aka parent) and that by staying on high alert and continually asking for reassurance, she could get her emotional security needs met. We also examined how her parents' divorce at a young age contributed to her internalizing the belief that intimacy is not safe and is "unpredictable." She confessed she had grown up shocked by her parents' separation because it seemed they had had the "perfect marriage" and "never fought." (More about why never fighting is actually a terrible sign later on in this book.)

Through our work together, Selena identified her anxious attachment triggers and attachment behaviors. Additionally, we unpacked her pattern of being attracted to emotionally unavailable men. It made sense; she chose partners who reflected her beliefs about love. When she selected emotionally unavailable men with a low tolerance for intimacy, these partners confirmed she had to "work hard for love" and that she was "too much." Once Selena had this awareness, she was able to let go of her old patterns. After coaching, she was able to begin her journey to embodying a securely attached woman and practicing securely attached dating. Ultimately, Selena attracted a healthy, stable, securely attached relationship into her life and was incredibly grateful for our work together.

Now let's examine the second attachment style.

ATTACHMENT STYLE #2: AVOIDANT ATTACHMENT
Definition
Avoidant attachment: I'm afraid I will lose myself and my independence if I allow myself to get close in a relationship. I have a fear of being suffocated and believe I need to be self-sufficient in order to prevent this from happening. I tend to distance myself

from my partner, and I spend the majority of my time investing in myself. I often interpret my partner's behaviors as signs of neediness and clinginess. I do not want my partner to depend on me. Relationships are often disappointing. If I get close to someone, I will likely let them down and disappoint them in some way.

Avoidant Attachment Behaviors

- Creates emotional distance through devaluing, hyperindependence, etc.
- Downplays their emotions and invalidates emotional experience
- Invalidates partners due to discomfort with emotions and/or conflict
- Struggles to maintain closeness, will "pull back" if feels too close
- Expects negative feedback from their partner
- Avoids difficult conversations
- Ends a relationship when it gets "too close"
- Engages in infidelity as a means to end a relationship/create distance
- Struggles to feel emotionally safe with others
- Hates to ask for help or depend on others for support

Avoidant Attachment Thoughts

"I must take care of myself and not depend on others."

"It's best if I keep my emotions to myself."

"I don't want someone who depends on me; I can't be a parent to my partner."

"I need to make sure my needs are met and that I get to do what I want."

"Am I even ready for commitment?"

"Am I settling? Is this person even good enough for me?"

"Do I *really* want the responsibility of a partner? What if I let them down?"

"I'm just bad at relationships…"

"I don't know if I even want a relationship. I will just focus on my career."

Have you struggled to let your walls down? Is there a drawbridge and a moat around your heart? (Or maybe an icebox where your heart used to be? Thanks for that gem of a metaphor, Omarion.) Perhaps your exes would describe you as cold, distant, and aloof. Or maybe you've found yourself unintentionally sabotaging great relationship after great relationship by pushing your partner away just when things start to get intimate. Cue: "Dang it! I know I shouldn't have slept with the cabana boy after my boyfriend asked me to marry him. Whoops!" The struggle with intimacy isn't because deep down you're a Grinch meant to live alone on a hill…it's much more complex than that.

What happens when intimacy becomes associated with pain and/ or disappointment? Let's explore my client Alice's experience to get a closer look at the avoidant attachment style.

Alice's Story

Like many women who enter the E.S.L. program, Alice was the child of emotionally unavailable alcoholic parents. Simply put, Alice was forced to become a parentified child in order to survive. She was responsible for her own well-being from a very young age. By age fifteen, she was having to scoop her father off the floor of the local bar and drive him home at 2 a.m. When Alice was sixteen, she comforted her mom when her dad ran off with his mistress. There was no space for her to express *her* needs or emotions, so she learned to ignore her own experience. Instead of validating her own emotions and needs, she was stuck in survival mode, constantly dissociated from her internal experience. If emotions surfaced, she pushed them aside.

Alice became a "star student" and achieved a perfect 4.0 GPA in both high school and college. She knew her ability to achieve and be productive was something she could control. And staying busy also helped her continue to ignore her emotions and needs. When it came to her love life, she frequently turned down dates and pushed potential partners away. She was "busy" and "didn't have time to date." Plus, no one was "on her level." The one time she did get fairly involved with someone, he ended up being a closet heroin addict, confirming her belief that relationships were just an energy-sucking waste of time. Alice could have lived the rest of her life scaling the corporate ladder and traveling the world with her girlfriends, but there was a slight problem. There was this small part of her that wanted to build a life with someone. Below her "independent woman, don't need no man" exterior, she desired the family life she never had as a kid. By the time I met her, she was near hopeless that this was possible for her, but she knew she needed to give love her best shot.

Inside of the E.S.L. program, Alice began to understand for the first time ever that her relationship blueprint was designed to keep her "safe" (and disconnected). Through our work together, she began to develop the securely attached version of herself and learn what it looked like for her to practice attachment strategies that kept her safe *and* allowed for intimacy. Slowly, she allowed dating to take up space in her life. She let her walls down and allowed a beautiful relationship to develop with an amazing, emotionally available man. She finally learned what it meant to be loved and to be safe. She learned to embody the empowered, secure, and loved woman that in the past had seemed like a fairytale.

Now let's look at attachment style #3.

ATTACHMENT STYLE #3: DISORGANIZED ATTACHMENT
Definition

Disorganized attachment: I desire intimacy and I am afraid of it. I feel I often take two steps forward in a relationship and then two steps back. I am both afraid of abandonment and afraid of my partner desiring too much closeness with me. I often do not understand my own behaviors in relationships and find I can be unpredictable at times. I tend to pendulum swing from desiring closeness with my partner to desiring extreme independence. I often misinterpret my partner's behaviors and they frequently express frustration with me being "hot and cold."

Disorganized Attachment Behaviors

- Creates chaos in relationships at times (often unconsciously)
- Lacks self-soothing skills and is emotionally volatile
- Practices a push-pull dynamic in relationships

- Seeks reassurance and independence simultaneously
- Has an extreme fear of rejection and abandonment
- Finds it difficult to trust others and struggles to trust self
- Is highly sensitive to partner's behaviors and mood
- Often switches between devaluing self and devaluing others

Disorganized Attachment Thoughts

"I'd like to date, but how can I trust anyone?"

"If I trust someone, they are likely to hurt me. I need to stay prepared to leave."

"If I threaten to leave the relationship, they can prove they love me by begging me to stay."

"I wish relationships weren't so emotionally draining and exhausting."

"My dating life is negatively impacting my career, my friendships, and my family relationships."

"I don't think I will ever be capable of being in a 'normal' relationship..."

"I want them to like me but not *too* much. And if they don't like me, I will find someone better immediately."

"People just want to use your vulnerability against you; they don't actually care."

Childhood trauma can have a major impact on your attachment

system. If your caregivers neglected you, were abusive in any way, or were simply unreliable, you may have developed traits of a disorganized attachment style. Disorganized attachment is also known as fearful-avoidant style, and it is the combination of both anxious and avoidant attachment. It makes sense, right? If you could not predict your caregiver's behavior, you needed to practice both anxious and avoidant tactics for survival. Disorganized attachment is one of the most painful ways of existing in relationships; it is filled with chaos, pain, and frustration. Often individuals with this attachment style feel like giving up on dating altogether and have almost lost all hope of having a great relationship. Let's take a look at Kara's story to learn more about a disorganized attachment style.

Kara's Story

Kara was deeply struggling when she came to the E.S.L. program. She said that her goals for the program were to learn how to regulate her emotions and put an end to the "shit show" that was her dating life. She expressed that she often dated men with substance use issues, and her latest boyfriend left her and immediately started dating one of her good friends. Kara was a mess as she sobbed her way through our initial session. She shared patterns of intense highs and lows in relationships and said that as soon as she got close to someone, she often felt she wanted to "flee the scene" immediately. She was ready to give up on dating entirely, and this program was her last hope. Luckily, I had helped women like Kara many times before, and I knew exactly how to help her.

As Kara went through the program, she began to develop clarity around the ways the abuse she experienced in childhood was sabotaging her love life. She learned that her father's emotionally abusive comments shaped her internal beliefs about herself and that she had developed a great deal of fear around intimacy and closeness. After releasing unhelpful beliefs rooted in trauma, Kara and I worked to help her tune in to the securely attached version of herself. Kara learned that when she changed her belief system and equipped herself with the tools to operate as securely attached, her relationship fears began to subside.

Halfway through the program, Kara shared that she was setting boundaries for the first time ever, learning to communicate assertively, and finally enjoying her dating life. Last I heard from her, she was dating a wonderful (emotionally available) guy, and they were traveling to Costa Rica together. More importantly, Kara shared that she finally felt at peace with *herself*. She learned to self-soothe for the first time ever, and her emotions no longer felt like tsunamis but more like calm baby waves at a SoCal beach. Kara had become empowered, secure, and loved; she was no longer fearful and hopeless. Stories like Kara's highlight the brain's resilience. We can *always* move toward secure attachment. As you may have guessed, secure attachment is the goal. Let's examine what that looks like.

ATTACHMENT STYLE #4: SECURE ATTACHMENT
Definition

Secure attachment: I can maintain my identity while becoming close to my partner. I value a close relationship with my partner and value my independence. I feel having close relationships is one of the most important things in life. I can tune in to and honor my boundaries. I can openly and honestly communicate my feelings and needs. I have capacity for my partner's needs, and I make space to offer them support. My partner adds value to my life and is there when I need them, and I know I do the same for them in return.

Secure Attachment Behaviors

- Practices open, honest, and direct communication
- Easily sets and maintains boundaries
- Maintains personal fulfillment and cocreates partner fulfillment
- Expresses reassurance and asks for reassurance as needed
- Easily expresses emotional experience
- Is open to hearing partner's experience and is open to their emotional experience
- Feels attuned to partner
- Shares emotional labor, cocreates secure attachment
- Exhibits independence instead of hyperindependence or codependence

Secure Attachment Thoughts

"I value my partner and the life we are building together."

"I appreciate my partner's strengths and the ways we work together as a team."

"My needs matter, and my partner's needs matter."

"How can I support my partner better?"

"How can I ask for what I need so that my partner can hear it?"

"What are ways I can take better care of myself, and how can I support my partner in taking better care of themself?"

"What do I want in my relationship?"

You know those people who seem to effortlessly navigate relationships and fall deeply in love with their "person"? Well, it's likely they have a secure attachment style. To take a closer look at secure attachment in action, let's get to know my friend Avery.

Avery's Story

I met Avery through a mutual friend. She was warm, funny, and engaging. I knew right away that I wanted to be friends with her. Avery was the owner of a successful waxing boutique in town, and she had the kind of presence that could make you feel at ease even if you were getting a Brazilian.

In getting to know Avery, she opened up about her marriage to her husband, Brad. She explained that she and Brad were "a team." Even though Avery had a one-year-old daughter and another kid on the way, with Brad's support, she still managed to run the waxing studio. She explained that she and Brad communicated well and always made sure they knew how to support one another, no matter what was going on in their busy lives. When Avery and I discussed her past dating history, she shared that she had never really had any "bad relationships." She explained that if someone wasn't treating her right, she would leave the relationship almost immediately. She chalked this up to seeing her parents stay happily married and in love for thirty years and knowing "how she deserved to be treated."

One thing I loved about Avery's story was her unshakable connection to her worth and standards. A main facet of secure attachment is deeply knowing your worthiness and immediately rejecting people/places/things who do not honor it. There was no "Oh yeah, I dated this one terrible guy who didn't value me for three years, and then when he cheated, I finally left" in her story. Avery lived her life with an awareness of what she deserved, and she effortlessly attracted it. Secure attachment will help ground you in knowing what you deserve and then aligning with the thoughts and behaviors to *actually back it up*. We can all learn from Avery's story, and also, we don't have to grow up as securely attached in order to become securely attached. As I've stated, *anyone* can learn to move toward secure attachment. And hey, you're reading this book, so you're off to a helluva start.

ATTACHMENT STYLES ON A CONTINUUM

Now that you know the four different attachment styles, it is important to acknowledge that we all have the capacity to *have traits of each of the four styles*. The reality is you may have a tendency to choose a certain attachment strategy based on the situation, the other person involved, and how well you've taken care of yourself. Now before you throw this book down in confusion, let me explain: think of your unique attachment style as being comprised of a percentage of each attachment style.

For example, you may find that 75 percent of the time, you are anxious and the other 25 percent, you are securely attached. Or perhaps you possess anxious, avoidant, and secure attachment traits. However, when you can pinpoint the style with which you identify most, this precious knowledge will help you understand your patterns in dating. When you can identify which of the attachment styles is framing your thinking and behavior, you can empower yourself to move toward secure attachment.

In order to prepare for what is to come in the next chapter, make sure you take the attachment style quiz below! I want you to understand your own attachment style. By reading this chapter, you may have guessed what yours is, but let's find out for sure.

EXERCISE #4: ATTACHMENT STYLE QUIZ

Go take my attachment style quiz here: www.drmorgancoaching. com/attachmentstylequiz.

Pro tip: come back to this quiz as needed. As you "do the work," you may find your percentage of time spent in secure attachment has increased. Look at you, healing and growing. Go you!

Congratulations! You are one of the few. You are taking your understanding of relationships to a new level, and it is going to pay huge dividends in your love life. Learning about your attachment style and identifying your unique attachment behaviors gives you a huge advantage in the game of love. You not only understand why you do what you do, but you also grasp why you are attracted to certain people. This awareness alone is incredibly powerful, and through my clients' experiences, I have witnessed hundreds of "light bulb" moments and feelings of relief as they've learned about attachment theory for the first time. Given that I am committed to helping you *radically* transform your dating life, I am going to take your understanding of attachment theory even further. In the upcoming chapter, you will learn how to *apply* attachment theory principles to your dating life. It is one thing to logically know what it looks like to show up securely attached;

it is entirely different to embody the securely attached woman in practice. In the next chapter, you will receive all of my best practices for embodying the securely attached version of you! I can't wait for you to take what you learn and apply it to your love life.

CHAPTER FIVE

ATTACHMENT THEORY IN ACTION

"I just don't understand why he won't text me back. I mean, I know he has his phone, and I know he read my messages. Why can't he take two seconds to respond?" Beth moaned as she sat across from me in the poorly decorated office lit by a blinking fluorescent light. At that time, I was still earning my clinical hours toward licensure and still dating emotionally unavailable men myself, so I knew all too well the pain she was talking about. Like any good therapist, I intently listened to her long, detailed stories of all the ways her love interest, Ben, was letting her down and causing her gut-wrenching anxiety. I validated how hurt she felt and agreed that Ben's behavior was terribly confusing.

Eventually, when I could get a word in, I asked Beth two very important questions: "What does this feeling remind you of? When was the first time in your life you felt that you were giving to a relationship, and it wasn't reciprocated?" Beth looked as though she had seen a ghost, and she responded with tears welled up in her eyes. "My dad," she said. Those two words began the real work for Beth. In the therapy sessions that followed, we waded through the ways she was failed as a child by her father. With each session, we began to unpack her relationship template and learn exactly how she came to develop an anxious attachment style. One of the important concepts I introduced to Beth during this work was "repetition compulsion."

REPETITION COMPULSION: THIS TIME IT WILL BE DIFFERENT!

Let me explain. This is not just a fancy term to make me sound educated. It is a term that explains an incredibly common unhealthy relationship dynamic that repeats itself until it is stopped. Repetition indicates the repeating of a pattern, and compulsion speaks to the inability to control the pattern, a pattern that repeats unconsciously and without your knowledge. Repetition compulsion boils down to this: you compulsively date your unfinished business, all the while unconsciously wishing for a different outcome. What it looks like is using old relationship templates in your current dating life, hoping that *this time* you will win over the affection of the unavailable person.

Even deeper in your unconscious fantasy is that if you have a different outcome this time, it will make up for all the times before when you didn't receive the love you needed. For example, if I can finally get the emotionally unavailable person to love me, it will make up for the love my father never gave me. It will prove that yes, I am good enough, and this time I was victorious in my efforts of doing whatever it takes to be loved. This unhealthy dynamic leads to women dating the same type of man over and over, hoping for a "miracle" outcome, and sadly, being disappointed every time when the outcome is the same. Ugh.

It's like going to the library every weekend, hoping there will be a rock concert. It's like flying Spirit Airlines repeatedly, hoping that one day it will feel like first-class Delta. It's like going to Walmart over and over, each time hoping that *this* will be the time you have a lovely shopping experience. Going to McDonald's and praying this time you will receive a perfectly cooked medium-rare steak. Or only buying Hyundai cars with the wish that you would finally be the owner of a Mercedes. You get the idea. It doesn't make *sense*, yet you do it anyway. Why? Repetition compulsion.

You get the point, right? If the inputs (the kind of guys you are dating) remain the *same*, the outputs (the heartbreak/bad relationships/bad dates) are the *same*. This simple science is completely overridden by our attachment systems and our unfinished business. And it wreaks havoc on your dating life. You're like, "Okay, I get it! Now how the heck do I quit dating my unfinished business?" The good news is I've already given you tools to do this. The relationship inventory, and the "Is This Serving You?" exercise from Chapter 1 will absolutely help you. And because I absolutely want you to completely rid your dating life of repetition compulsion, you will have access to a bonus exercise, "Healing Unfinished Business," which is available to you at www.drmorgancoaching. com/lovegmagnetgifts.

ERIC AND ANNIE'S STORY

To further illustrate attachment theory in action, I'd like to introduce you to Eric and Annie. I began working with Eric and Annie in couples therapy, and it was clear to me early on that, ultimately, the role of this therapy work was to facilitate a separation. In other words, this couple was not staying together, and it was my job to help them end the relationship as peacefully as possible. They were both late twenties, well educated, and good-looking people. They looked like a perfectly matched couple by physical appearances and were both warm to me upon meeting them. With a deeper look into their relationship dynamic, I learned that Eric displayed disorganized attachment patterns and Annie had high levels of anxious attachment. Eric struggled with hearing Annie, so much so that during our sessions, he would keep his eyes closed. He could not look at his partner during emotional discussions; it was too much for him. He was overwhelmed and uncomfortable.

Additionally, Eric had started an "emotional affair" with a coworker. You see, with his avoidant attachment behaviors of not feeling able to open up emotionally to his partner, he was forced to find other sources of emotional connection. Annie began feeling less close to Eric, and when he refused to move in with her after two and a half years of dating, her anxious attachment patterns went into overdrive. She knew something was wrong, and she searched until she found the proof. The proof was in Eric's journal, where he had written about his relationship with his coworker. Annie was devastated and was convinced the relationship was over. In the aftermath of Annie telling Eric the relationship must end, *Eric's* anxious attachment patterns and deep fear of abandonment became activated, and he begged Annie to go to therapy and work on things. He promised he would change. And that's how they ended up in my office.

Annie had never been to therapy before, and frankly, she didn't want to be there. Additionally, she was very angry and emotionally dysregulated. There were sessions where she begged Eric to put her "out of her misery" and just break up with her already. Eric refused to give up and tried to be the best client he could by doing all the homework I gave the couple. Luckily, I introduced them to attachment theory, and they began to understand their patterns. Annie began to learn how to "self-soothe" and move toward secure attachment so that she could communicate to Eric more effectively. Eric was connecting the dots to his childhood and his current relationship template. Things were clicking, and they were making progress. There were even a few sessions where I thought they might surprise me and stay together.

Months into therapy and approximately sixteen sessions deep, Eric appeared to our session with a letter in hand and asked if he could read it. Annie and I encouraged him to do so. Hands shaking and tears streaming down his face, he began to read. The letter detailed all the ways that he had failed Annie, and all the ways that he simply could not give her what she needed. At the end, he framed the breakup this way: "I need to work on me. I am too broken for you. You deserve so much better." After he read the letter, he left the session. Annie sat there in shock. She looked up at me and asked, "Now what?"

What happened next is by all means not a common practice in therapy. I took Annie on as an individual client. This was after careful consideration and consultation, and oddly enough, a blessing from Eric. Long story short, I helped Annie slowly heal and move toward secure attachment. We examined where her beliefs came from and rewired her belief system at her core. The beautiful thing is that I had the privilege of witnessing her growth as she attracted and dated a securely attached man. Someone who had high levels of emotional availability, offered reassurance, and was ready for emotional investment. She fell in love with a man who did what he said he was going to do, who loved her deeply, and who knew how to reciprocate effort.

I watched Annie go from sobbing on the therapy couch, covered in Kleenex whilst trying to connect with a partner who wouldn't even open his eyes, to blissfully happy in a securely attached partnership with a man who was crazy about her. Witnessing Annie's transformation only further cemented what I knew to be true: women need the science of attachment theory to change their dating lives. It is an absolute game changer when understood and applied. Additionally, I want to point out that Annie seemed to be a completely new person in her new relationship. When Eric had called her "too much" and "crazy," it exacerbated her ways of being; she had been in love with an emotionally unavailable partner. It is true that who we become in relationships can vary significantly according to who we are dating. This book is one step toward embodying secure attachment and learning to date intentionally. You can have relationship experiences you've never had before. Once again, I remind you: securely attached love, reciprocal love, and love that shows up *is* available to you.

ATTACHMENT THEORY MEETS MINDFULNESS SELF-COMPASSION

I want you to realize this: knowledge of attachment theory will only help you if you're willing to apply it and integrate it into your life. The knowledge alone will do you absolutely no good if you're not going to integrate it into your ways of being and thinking in relationships. It does nothing to know about driving a car unless you actually drive, right? Researching exercises and learning about fitness will not increase your physical health. You gotta get those running shoes on, girl! So, I want to arm you with the concept of "mindfulness self-compassion meets attachment theory." For short, I will call it MSC X AT. Let me break this down for you. We need to practice both mindfulness self-compassion and attachment theory in action to move toward a secure attachment style.

Mindfulness self-compassion is designed to help you notice, acknowledge, and accept your automatic attachment strategy and then intentionally (and with compassion) move you to the securely attached version of yourself. Let me walk you through an example here. I notice my partner has not texted me back. It's been three hours, and he usually texts me back within thirty minutes. I start to feel emotionally dysregulated: anxious, nauseated, beginning to sweat. The thoughts in my head are my worst-case scenario relationship fears coming true. What if he's no longer attracted to me? What if he doesn't want to hang out anymore? What if after six months of dating, he's decided he'd rather get back together with his ex than continue dating me?

At this moment, first I need mindfulness self-compassion. I place my hand over my heart, breathe deep into my belly, and acknowledge that my anxious attachment style has hijacked my brain. I send myself so much love in the moment and say something like, "I hear you, anxious attachment. I know you are trying to help me, except all you are actually doing is causing me massive amounts of stress and not helping at all. Morgan, I am sorry this feels so hard right now. You are so worthy of love and so deserving of support. I want you to know you are enough as you are, and you are showing up the best you can." Next, I need to move toward the securely attached version of me.

The next part of this process is realigning with the securely attached version of myself. I say to myself, "What does it look like for you to feel supported in this moment? How does the securely attached you show up in this situation? What do you need in order to help you move toward secure attachment right now?" In the example I provided, this could be as simple as fifteen minutes spent journaling, taking a walk, and repeating secure attachment affirmations. The key is to do your very best to learn to realign with the securely attached you before interacting with your partner.

Think of times in the past where your attachment system was spiraling out of control, and you decided to lash out at your partner or reach out to your partner to save you from your own emotional chaos. None of those attempts worked. Am I right? When we are learning to emotionally regulate and move toward secure attachment, we have to learn to do it for ourselves. If I'm spiraling into feelings of not being good enough, old beliefs that all of my relationships fail, or gut feelings of wanting to burn all of my relationships to the ground, this is not the time to attempt to interact with my partner. Work toward intentional communication by supporting yourself with realignment to a secure attachment style *before* you engage with your partner. At the end of this chapter, you will find the "Secure You" exercise, where I help you develop massive amounts of clarity on who exactly is the securely attached version of you so that you can effortlessly realign with her as needed.

For the Mindfulness Self-Compassion meditation and more, please visit: www.drmorgancoaching.com/lovemagnetgifts.

EXERCISE #5: "SECURE YOU"

It is time to get clear on the securely attached version of yourself. Answer these questions in your journal:

1. How do I feel when I am securely attached? What emotions come up for me? Examples: peaceful, safe, content, loved…
2. What are ten "I" statements that define who I am when I am

in a securely attached state? Examples: I am confident and kind. I easily set boundaries, and I honor my needs. I express my emotions, and I feel open to receiving love. I am honest about my relationship standards, and I communicate my non-negotiables. Now it is your turn! Write out ten statements that define the securely attached version of you!

Now that you have a clear vision for the securely attached version of you and how she shows up in relationships, it is up to you to do your best to realign with her again and again. In moments when it feels easiest to do what you have always done and slip into your old ways of being, can you pause, use mindfulness self-compassion, and realign with the securely attached version of you? Of course, there will be times where your old relationship patterns will take over. You may find yourself slipping into your old attachment behaviors, and I want you to know that is completely *okay*. You have not "failed." When an old way of being presents itself, it is simply an opportunity to practice realigning with the securely attached version of yourself. Experiment, notice, and always, always practice self-compassion when noticing ways of being that no longer serve you.

Use your "Secure You" list as a North Star for secure attachment. Over time, you will notice it gets easier and easier to naturally show up as the securely attached version of you. Your realignment will take minutes instead of days, your need to realign will go from daily to monthly, and slowly but surely, you will begin to embody the most securely attached and confident version of yourself. You've got this, babe! Now onward to the next part of the book, where you will take all you have learned about embodying secure attachment and combine it with the very best relationship tools, dating mindset, and communication frameworks! Get your swiping finger ready, and let's go on to Part 3 of this book: "Securely Attached Dating, Securely Attached Relationships"!

PART THREE

SECURELY ATTACHED DATING, SECURELY ATTACHED RELATIONSHIPS

CHAPTER SIX

DATING AS THE SECURELY ATTACHED WOMAN: GET OUT THERE AND ATTRACT A GREAT RELATIONSHIP!

James arrived on time, pulled out my chair for me as I sat down for dinner, and asked really great questions that seemed to indicate he genuinely wanted to get to know me. As the night went on, he smiled and shared how much he liked my caring nature and admired that I valued my relationship with my family. Inside my head I thought, *What the hell is happening? Is this guy actually listening to me and openly interested in me? And how is he this good-looking and not a jerk?* I was having one of my very first securely attached dating experiences, and it felt *different*. James wanted to get to know me, he wanted to take things slow, and he was interested in a serious relationship. His intentions were clear, and his communication was easy to understand. He always texted me back, and he did what he said he was going to do. When you start to embody the securely attached woman, you might feel as if all of the securely attached men must have suddenly fallen from the sky! You will ask, "Where have all these men been?" The truth is, they have been there all along, but your attachment style did not let you feel attracted to them. Sis, it is your turn to become attracted to securely attached partners. It is your time to step into relationships that feel good and emotionally safe. This part of the book is going to help you feel unstoppable when it comes to dating and attracting your securely attached soulmate.

As a matter of fact, I'm raising my kombucha bottle to you right now, honey! Why, you ask? Because you've made it to the part of the book where the rubber meets the freaking road. You are at the place where very shortly, you will be ready to get out into the magical world of dating and apply everything you've learned. In Part 3 of this book, I am going to give you the mindset shifts and practical tools you need to date from a confident and securely attached place. Now that you understand your attachment style, and you are getting acquainted with your securely attached self, you are completely ready to venture back out into the dating world.

This is going to be fun! And enlightening, because let's be honest, no one ever teaches you how to date in a healthy and sustainable way. Get your highlighter out, take notes, and buckle up. We're about to look at dating in a way you've never seen before. We're going to turn you into an educated, intentional, and *conscious* dater. Think of me as your healthy relationship fairy godmother. And for God's sake, put away the Halsey playlist and bag of Cheetos, girl! Trust me. We're going to learn to make dating *fun*. Do you know why it is so very important to make dating fun? Because *when you enjoy something, you stay persistent.* You stick with it. And when it comes to dating, I'm not going to guarantee that you will read these next chapters, set the book down, and then *boom*, your Prince Charming will magically appear in your living room. Dating takes time, and there's some truth to the idea that it's a "numbers game." But you deserve to enjoy the process so that you will stay persistent and ultimately attract the relationship you deserve. You've got this, and I've got you. Let's go!

THERE IS NO FAILURE IN DATING

It has been said that an expert is someone who makes all the mistakes that can be made in a very narrow field. Lucky for you, I have made just about every possible mistake there is to be made when it comes to dating. And through all of it, I have learned this: failure in dating does not exist. "Failure" is simply learning and growth. Why is it that when a relationship ends, we are conditioned to believe we have *failed*? We reluctantly delete all the cute couple photos off our social media accounts (and proceed to post hot revenge selfies—am I right?), all the while fearing the judgment that will surely come from "another failed relationship." Here's the reality: no one's opinion of your journey to love matters but your own. What if we saw relationships as experiences? What if we viewed relationships as *vehicles for growth*?

When we commit to something, we accept there may be failure. Have you committed to having a great relationship? Have you "burned the boats" on this dream, or is there part of you that is still afraid of things "not working out" and you're letting that voice keep you on the sidelines of love? Girl, you deserve to get in the game. You deserve to know that if you truly desire a great relationship, it is available to you. Once you have committed to this and accept that a relationship is available to you, you will accept all "failure" as simply experience that is getting you closer to your great relationship. Remember this phrase: "rejection is redirection." When you are being "rejected" in a relationship, you are simply being redirected to the great relationship that is meant for you.

As humans, we are meaning-making creatures. Anytime a relationship doesn't work out, you get to decide the meaning you assign to this experience. To ensure a healthy dating mindset, be intentional with the meaning you assign to relationships that didn't work out. "A big waste of time" label will not serve you. Try "a learning experience that caused me to self-reflect" or "an experience that helped me gain clarity on what I truly want."

BE A LOVE SCIENTIST

Okay, time to put on your lab coat. Yes, it can be hot pink, silk, lacy, or just plain white. Whatever tickles your fancy, go for it, girl. You need to understand this: when you are dating, you are a *love scientist.* You are gathering data about the relationship that is right for you. And when you are gathering data (aka dating), you are learning about the other person and, even more importantly, learning about *how you feel* with the other person. Do you feel anxious? Do you feel heard and valued? Or do you feel devalued and unappreciated?

The other thing about gathering data is this: you can't run one single experiment and then violà! You've found the results you need! Anyone can understand that experiments must be run again and again, and data must be collected over time.

When you are dating, you need to gather data until the results you get are reliable and consistent. He's charming, funny, and a good listener on date number one? Oh, that's great, but it's *one date*. How is he on date seventeen, after he's had a rough day at work, and you just accidentally spilled wine on his lap? How is he during rush-hour traffic when you're late to his friend's birthday party? You need to gather the data on someone so that you'll know if they are worth the emotional investment.

Your emotional investment is *precious*, more precious than gold. You need to value your emotional investment and treat it with the highest respect. You cannot give it away freely, nor should you hoard it. You get to learn to invest with intention and with intelligence. A partner needs to earn your emotional investment and earn your vulnerability. Allow it to be gradual. Ensure it is reciprocal. And guard your heart.

Let me throw a scenario at you. Let's say you're investing in the stock market and you're ready to go all in. Your beloved grandmother just passed away and left you half of her life savings because she wanted you to be financially comfortable. You have this strong desire to create a secure financial future for yourself and invest your grandmother's hard-earned cash with the utmost care. If someone were to come to you and say, "Oh my gosh, you need to invest in XYZ stock because I know it is going to go up!" Would you take all of your money and invest in that stock right away? No. No, you wouldn't. You would learn about the stock, about the values of the company, and if you liked what you learned, you might invest a little capital and see how it did. It would be *crazy* to blindly invest all of your life savings into a stock you knew nothing about, right? Well, so many people approach relationships this way. When presented with a new relationship, they blindly invest their emotional energy without having gathered any data. And if I had to pick, I'd say your emotional energy is, in fact, even more valuable than money, so in my book, you'd be better off gambling on the stock market than with your precious emotional energy.

EXPECTATIONS VERSUS STANDARDS

Let's create an understanding of expectations versus standards. For the purposes of this book, I am going to define expectations as anytime your brain is trying to "fill in the blanks." This means anytime you are about to go on a date with a hot guy you matched with on Bumble and you find yourself thinking, *OMG, this guy could be the ONE! I mean he's tall, he's funny, and we both love the L.A. Lakers! I just know this date will go well.* Expectations are anytime you make assumptions about how a relationship will progress, what the person will be like, or *how you are going to feel* about the relationship. Expectations are very common coming from my anxiously attached folks, as the need to predict and control is very high. Okay, got that?

Let's move on, my conscious dating intern. Next up, what are dating standards? Your standards are a clearly defined set of values and nonnegotiables that you have for your relationship. These can include such items as healthy communication, respect, desire for physical intimacy, and growth mindset. The standards that are most important to you are unique to you. No two individuals will have exactly the same standards in the same order. Your standards are rooted in a deep knowing of what *you* need for a healthy, fulfilled relationship. Side note: our partner cannot meet *all* of our needs. Be intentional about the core needs and standards you have for your romantic partner. Take out a pen and paper and write out your top five standards right now.

Okay, now that we have a working definition of standards, let's apply this to dating. You need to drop expectations and hold firmly to your standards. When you are a love scientist, you are collecting data to determine: *does this person meet my standards?* If we let our expectations blur our vision, the data collection is contaminated with assumptions, and the results are not accurate. You need clear standards, no expectations, and patient data collection.

CURIOSITY IS HOT

But Dr. Morgan, if I don't have expectations when dating, what should I have instead? Well, I am really glad you asked that question. The answer is curiosity. Curiosity is your superpower! As a love scientist, having curiosity will greatly benefit your data collection, make the whole dang dating process so much more fun, and ultimately help you attract the partner who is meant for you. So yeah, be curious because it is a dating superpower.

Here's why curiosity is so powerful:

- It relaxes you.
- It helps you truly get to know the person you're dating (without expectations blurring your vision).
- It allows you to release tension/stress/anxiety and just have fun in the present moment.
- It makes you a magnet for what is meant for you (if we're placing too many expectations/making too many assumptions, we might throw off what the universe is trying to send our way).
- It removes blocks/expectations/assumptions.
- It is a welcoming, accepting, and warm energy that allows others to also be curious about you (and this energy is confident and very attractive).

So how do I practice being curious? You can start practicing now. Even if it's with your friends or your poor unsuspecting neighbor. I want you to ask yourself this question: "How can I *be in the presence of* this person?" When we are in the presence of another person, we first commit to being fully present. Second, we are tuned in. Third, we ask questions that we genuinely want to know the answer to. Are you tired of first dates that feel like job interviews? Girl, me too, and trust me, so is everyone you are going on dates with. Ask the questions you genuinely want to know the answer to. And then notice this: is the curiosity reciprocated? Do they want to know about you, just as much as you want to know about them?

Good signs someone is reciprocally interested in you are when they say things like, "I am so interested in getting to know you. I am so curious about you. I can't wait to hear more about you." All too often, we can become comfortable with people who prefer to talk about themselves and who express little interest in us. This is the side effect of an anxious attachment style, low self-worth, or recovering codependency. You know someone is curious about you when they ask good questions and they intently listen to your answers. They are engaged and tuned in. Curiosity is sexy!

YOU MUST HAVE AN OPEN PALM

If you were trying to catch a bird with your hand, would you fill it with the nicest birdseed, wait for a bird to land, and then squeeeeze the bird till its eyes popped out? You know the bird would *never* come back to you as soon as it got free, right? What about this approach? You say you REALLY want a bird in your hand. It's all you want, and having that bird in your hand is the only thing missing in your life. Yet, you are not holding out your palm, you have no birdseed, and you're on a couch watching Netflix where, guess what, there are exactly *zero* birds in your environment.

Attracting a great relationship requires us to have an open palm. If we "squeeze the bird," we cause it to feel trapped and want to fly away as soon as it can. If we make no effort and don't even have birdseed, we will never attract a bird. In this example, an anxious attachment style is squeezing the bird, and an avoidant style is not leaving the couch. Secure attachment means you hold an open palm with birdseed, and then when a bird lands, you welcome it and have no desire to force it to stay. You leave your palm open, and if the bird likes your birdseed and you like the bird, you will continue the relationship.

When it comes to relationships, we have false beliefs about control. We think if we do the right things, say the right things, hold on tightly (or pretend we don't care), we can make sure we hold on to the relationship we want. The great relationship that is right for you requires no game playing, no tactics, and no control. It requires that you show up with an open palm, capacity, and curiosity. You know I've talked about curiosity, but what about capacity? Well, let's talk about the truth about capacity.

A NOTE ABOUT CAPACITY

I need you to know something: *you can love someone in all the right ways, and they simply may not have the capacity to show up and love you back.* You can have the healthiest approach to love and come from a place of wholeness, and the person you love may not be able to meet you halfway. Capacity is the ability to emotionally give to someone else. The ability to water the relationship and help it grow. The ability to be present, to love, and to hold space. There are many humans who would love to have capacity for healthy love, but they simply do not. And when in a relationship, they must ask themselves, "Can I work on myself and create the capacity needed to help this relationship thrive, or shall I exit gracefully knowing I cannot provide what this relationship deserves in order to grow?" There are many reasons why people lack capacity. Unhealed relational trauma is one of the primary reasons, along with unresolved past romantic relationships and attachment wounds. This is partially why the work you are doing in this book is so important. You want to be able to *develop* your capacity to love well, and for many of us, this involves an intentional effort to heal. Cheers to you for making the effort; it will pay off immensely!

When a relationship ends due to lack of capacity from a partner, you will likely blame yourself at first. This is human nature. When we are rejected, we seek to understand why. Although knowing why never actually helps with the pain, somehow we've tricked ourselves into thinking it will. If I just knew *why*, then I could change it. Save yourself from this thought spiral as much as you can. I've labeled it the "relationship autopsy"—and trust me, I could have a PhD in "relationship autopsy," given how many I've conducted in my day.

Capacity is a force outside of two individuals. It is oftentimes something we are not aware of until we are in the relationship itself. It begs the question: Can I show up and love this person the way they deserve and need to be loved? Am I the person for this role? How do I feel when giving of myself? Can I maintain the ways that I give to myself as I give to another?

The beautiful thing? There are so many people out there right now who *do* have capacity and who would absolutely love to love you in the ways you need to be loved. There are so many people who would be thrilled to date you. People who want to learn from you and grow with you. There are people who want to roll up their sleeves and do the work of building a healthy, great relationship with you. I promise.

PACING/INVESTMENT POOL/INTIMACY ONION

Most women I work with either rush headfirst into a relationship, or they never even dip their toe in. Take a second and ask yourself which is usually your pattern. Do you avoid emotional investment like the plague, or are you picturing your wedding on date two? Do you know which approach you usually take? Okay, good! Now I want you to picture a pool. This isn't just any pool; this is the emotional investment pool. The deeper you go, the more emotionally invested you are in the relationship. Dive in headfirst without knowing what's there, and you just might end up with a concussion. Anytime you enter into a new relationship, whether it is conscious or unconscious, you decide if you want to emotionally invest. My goal is to help you make the decision to emotionally invest in a conscious, intentional, and safe decision.

Here's the deal: a relationship needs to earn your vulnerability and your emotional investment. If you are in the deep end of the emotional investment pool and your partner is merely dipping his toe in, should you really be in the deep end? Has the relationship earned that depth of emotional investment from you? The answer is hell no, girl! As you deepen your emotional investment, a level of secure attachment is required. If the secure attachment is not there to support the investment, you must intentionally discuss this with your partner.

One of the most important pieces about the emotional investment pool is that you deserve to know where each of you is in the pool at all times. If I'm in the deep end and my partner is dipping his toe in, I need to know that. If I'm sitting on the edge of the pool and don't actually want to get in, my partner needs to know that. The reality is that as you are building a new relationship, you will not often be in the exact same part of the pool. However, you will want to know where each partner is at and do your best to stay relatively close. If I'm four feet in, my partner would ideally be somewhere between three and five feet in.

Remember, a partner must *earn* your vulnerability. You have so many layers to you. Painful experiences that have shaped you. Dreams that you hold near and dear to your heart. Fears, anxieties, desires, and goals. There is no one quite like you on this planet. You are deserving of sharing who you are at a pace that feels comfortable to you. As you invest more emotionally, your level of vulnerability grows as well. Typically, I see one of two problems when women are dating: either they share *everything* all at once, or they share very little and never allow someone to get to know them. If we think about the metaphor of your heart as an onion, and you can picture the layers, you must be willing to peel the layers slowly to develop the intimacy that you desire. You must also be willing to support your partner in peeling the layers of their heart. Peeling onions can cause tears, and it's not always easy. You must be gentle with one another and take your time in peeling the layers. Vulnerability is a precious gift; do not give away all of who you are at once. Savor it. Take in the data of how your partner reacts when you share. Can they support more layers coming off? Can you wade deeper into the emotional investment pool?

RED FLAGS, YELLOW FLAGS, AND GREEN FLAGS, OH MY!

Okay, so you've got your sexy lab coat on, and you understand you need to be a love scientist. The question is: what are you looking for? I've got you covered, girl. I've developed a list of red, yellow, and green flags! One thing I want you to note is that as you gain trust with yourself and you learn to tune in to how you feel, you will rely on this list less and less. When you are focused on how you want to feel and making sure your relationships support those feelings, you rely less on tactical lists and more and more on gut feelings. However, early on in "doing the work," lists like the one below can be very helpful.

Please note: Red flags are things we can give feedback on, but it is unlikely there is much room for improvement. A yellow flag is an opportunity for feedback, and you are encouraged to provide that feedback to your partner. And green flags mean "Send that love boat full steam ahead! The data is looking good!"

RED FLAGS

- Communication is inconsistent (completely falls off the radar for a week or more).
- You don't feel you can be yourself at all.
- There is no space in the conversation for you to share how you feel.
- You feel invalidated, and he says things like "you're crazy,""that's not true," etc.

- He uses manipulation and says things like, "I will do this if you do that" or "I will only love you if you ____." (RUN!)
- Says, "All of my exes are crazy."
- Has a terrible relationship with all family members.
- Thinks therapy is B.S. and that people with mental health issues are "weak."
- Puts you down constantly (even in a joking way).
- Asks you for huge favors early on: "Can I borrow money? Can I borrow your car? Can you help me move this weekend?"
- Exhibits "love bombing" behaviors—displays of love and affection that are not in line with the amount of time spent in the relationship. Examples: saying "I love you" on the second date, showering you with gifts, placing you on a pedestal with excessive compliments.
- Does not honor your boundaries (physical, time, preference, etc.).
- Uses any kind of hurtful language or physical abuse.
- Says, "If you loved me, you would _____."

YELLOW FLAGS

- Arrives late to the first date.
- Makes a few jokes that are meant to be funny but hurt your feelings.
- Shares that he has prioritized his career and that this is why he "hasn't found the one."
- Talks a bit more about himself than he listens to you, but he does ask a few questions about you.
- Says he has a terrible relationship with both parents but gets along with at least one family member.
- Drinks more than five drinks in a three-hour time frame and swears "he doesn't usually drink like this."

- Shares that he struggles to open up and finds it hard to express himself, but he wants to work on it.
- Explains that his last relationship took a toll on him, and he feels he is finally recovering.
- Is a slow texter—it takes a while to respond, but he typically does get back to you.
- Wants to emotionally invest quickly—invites you to meet family and/or friends prior to the sixth date.

GREEN FLAGS

- Is an open, honest, and direct communicator.
- Seems genuinely interested in getting to know you.
- Communicates well and offers reassurance easily.
- Has stated he is open to building a serious relationship.
- Reports great relationships with family and friends.
- Listens intently and validates how you feel.
- Remembers details from your conversations.
- Welcomes physical touch and is curious about your love language.
- Honors your boundaries and is comfortable spending time alone and together.

EXERCISE #6: IDENTIFY THE FLAGS OF YOUR LAST RELATIONSHIP

There's no better way to learn than to apply your knowledge immediately! Knowing what you now know, after reaching this point in the book and having just reviewed red/yellow/green relationship flags, I have a powerful exercise for you. I want you to take your last significant relationship that ended and identify the red, yellow, and green flags that were present. Get your journal ready, and make your own table that looks like this:

RELATIONSHIP WITH (INSERT NAME)

RED FLAGS	YELLOW FLAGS	GREEN FLAGS

Now ask yourself these questions:

"What got in the way of seeing these flags clearly?"

"How would I react differently now, if I were in this relationship today?"

I want to give you another hug and a high five! You have learned so much about dating and showing up as the securely attached version of yourself who knows how to attract a great relationship! I see you doing the work. Congratulations, beautiful! You are on your way to intentionally ever after. What is intentionally ever after, you ask? It is when you get to intentionally create a securely attached relationship that *lasts*. One that deepens and strengthens over time. Once you attract a great relationship, you need all the tools that will support you in *maintaining* it. Lucky for you, I've got you covered in the next chapter, where you will start off with learning all about intentionally ever after and the modern woman's securely attached relationship manifesto. From there, you will learn all about a healthy communication framework for navigating conflict, and so much more! The next chapter is everything you wish someone would have taught you about relationships.

CHAPTER SEVEN

INTENTIONALLY EVER AFTER: WRITE YOUR OWN LOVE STORY

Stella deeply loved her boyfriend. They had been together for five years, and she was ready for a ring. She was thirty-two, for crying out loud! Why hadn't Tyler proposed yet? She sat on the blue velvet couch in my La Jolla office with a look of desperation on her face and tears welling up in her eyes. She was at a turning point. Should she leave the relationship, or make her feelings known to Tyler? She didn't want to end things with Tyler, and yet she deeply needed reassurance that they were in fact intentionally building a life together. Through our work together, Stella ultimately braved the conversation with Tyler and got to the root of his avoidance of marriage. It turned out that Tyler was afraid he "wasn't good enough" for Stella, and specifically, he feared he wouldn't be able to financially provide in the ways he felt Stella deserved. Through Stella's work in the therapy room, and by using the tools you will find in this chapter, the couple managed to heal and strengthen their relationship. Tyler did ultimately propose, and as far as I know, they are a securely attached and happily married couple. All because Stella was willing to do the work.

The tools and frameworks you will learn in this chapter have saved marriages, deepened commitments, and generally helped hundreds of people have great relationships. Why this material is not taught in high school is beyond me. There are very few of us who have family systems that model securely attached healthy relationships, and Lord knows relationships in the media typically set a horrible example. Trust me, even if you have never personally witnessed a healthy, securely attached relationship, you can create one. And this chapter will help you do it! Get ready to take in knowledge that will positively impact your relationships for the rest of your life.

INTENTIONAL RELATIONSHIPS/CONSCIOUS COUPLING

What does the word "intentional" mean? To put it in the simplest of terms, intentional means on purpose. We are leaving the age of marriage for survival, reproduction for evolution's sake, and coupling up because it's "what our parents did." There is a revolution of conscious coupling. You get to decide if you want to welcome in this new relationship paradigm or stick with the old "partnership for partnership's sake" model. The beautiful thing is the shift from "I need a relationship" to "I want a relationship." The days of having a relationship template forced upon you are over. You can decide what kind of relationship you want, and *you can create it.*

Here's the deal: the old ways of being in romantic relationships did not require self-reflection, "doing the work," or healing ourselves. There were clearly defined roles, low expectations, and plenty of unsatisfied people who just thought marriage was what they were "supposed to do." What we know now is that the level to which we are willing to do the work will align with the level of depth and connection we can experience with others. In other words, if you would like a conscious, connected, securely attached relationship, it is available to you. It simply requires intentional investment and conscious coupling. We get to write our own love stories, where we live happily, intentionally ever after.

The reality is that women can exist in today's society as single women and *thrive*. There is no need for a partner. The healed woman knows she does not need a partner, and she also acknowledges *that she deserves to have what she wants*. From a place of desire and clarity, the empowered, secure, and loved woman can create the conscious relationship she desires. She does not need permission, and she does not need to follow roles predetermined by society. She creates what feels good to her and honors her worthiness to receive the kind of relationship she wants. She wants a partnership, someone she can grow with. She wants someone to have her back and someone who is not afraid to call her out. Someone to lean on and someone to push her. She desires deep connection, passion, and *freedom*. A conscious relationship that is capable of honoring her independence while simultaneously drawing her in close. She has no time for games. She knows she deserves what she wants.

DIALOGUE AND CONFLICT NAVIGATION

Now that we have talked about making sure you are aligned with the securely attached version of yourself before you communicate with your partner, let's dive into how in the world you can navigate conflict and have tough conversations with your partner. You've shown up to the party with your best dress on (aka secure attachment), but now, how do you dance so that you don't stomp on your partner's toes? Well, my friends, the answer is that you must understand the power of dialogue. I promise you this: if you take nothing else from this book, the practice of using dialogue in your relationships will be a game-changing, relationship-healing, life-altering experience. This is the communication framework that should be mandatory in schools. This framework has saved marriages, deepened relationships, and brought peace to families, workplaces, and schools. Listen up!

TODD AND JULIE'S STORY

There was a couple I worked with, Todd and Julie. They were high achieving, mid-thirties, and loved one another deeply. The concern they presented with in therapy was that they could not agree on whether or not to move in together. They had been together five years, they loved one another, and wanted to deepen their relationship. Yet Todd could not bring himself to look at houses with Julie. As we began to get deeper into the work, we learned that Todd used a mixture of anxious and secure attachment behaviors, and Julie typically showed up as avoidantly attached. Anytime there was an argument, Todd did not feel emotionally safe to express himself. Through deep work and the use of dialogue, we began to learn that Julie's unconscious protection of herself through avoidant attachment behaviors and Todd's high needs for reassurance were sabotaging the deepening of their union.

Todd and Julie were required to learn the dance of conflict navigation to save their relationship. To provide a framework that supported them, I taught them how to use intentional dialogue. The dialogue framework they learned in our sessions together enabled them to express their core fears, desires, and emotions. They learned to see one another as emotional beings with past relationship experiences that shaped their fears. They learned to offer reassurance about the things that really mattered. Within six months of working together, they had learned a whole new way of communicating. They became closer than ever before and decided to purchase a home together. They went on to decide to get married and have a child. The deepening of their union was all possible because they decided to lean in and learn to intentionally communicate.

EXERCISE #7.1: DIALOGUE 101

Let's learn how to dialogue. Right now, I need you to know *you can do this.* No matter how poor your communication has been in the past, you can always learn new ways of communicating. I am going to make it super simple for you.

In dialogue, there is always a "sender" and a "receiver." The sender's job is to communicate their experience using "I" statements, and sharing the emotions they feel. The receiver's only job is to make sure the sender feels heard. Notice I did not say the receiver's job is to get defensive, invalidate, or judge. Their only job is to ensure the sender feels heard.

There are four parts to the dialogue process, and of course I am going to break it down for you right here. Keep in mind when you sit down to have a dialogue, you want to be able to look at one another, and you may even want to hold hands if you feel comfortable doing so. When first learning how to use dialogue, you may feel more comfortable having this kind of conversation while walking or sitting side by side. Ideally, you'll want to work up to a dialogue practice where you are looking directly at one another.

PART ONE: THE INVITATION

Dialogue is a time for you and your partner to deeply connect and understand one another, and frankly, it is sacred. It is not something you do while brushing your teeth, watching TV, or when you're exhausted from a twelve-hour shift. To have successful dialogue, you need to invite your partner to communicate when you can both be present. There is never a perfect time, but make it a time where distractions are minimal and you're relatively well rested. The rule with an invitation is that if either of you is unavailable at the time proposed, you must agree upon a new time.

PART TWO: SENDER COMMUNICATES TO RECEIVER; RECEIVER VALIDATES

The first person to "send" will typically be the person who is presenting the conflict. The sentence structures to consider using are: "I felt _____ when you...," "I feel _____ when xyz happens," "The story I'm telling myself is _____." The point of being the sender is to fully communicate your experience of the conflict. What did you feel emotionally? What were the thoughts you had, even if logically you know they weren't true? You want to be vulnerable here so that you can move through the conflict and avoid letting resentment build. The receiver will validate. Their only job is to listen and repeat back what they heard. For example, they would say things like, "I hear you felt hurt when I was thirty minutes late. The story you were telling yourself is that I don't care about you or our relationship."

PART THREE: SWITCH ROLES—SENDER COMMUNICATES TO RECEIVER; RECEIVER VALIDATES

When it is time to switch roles, it is important to note that this is not an opportunity to get defensive. The format remains the same: "I" statements and validation. Then you want to continue to switch roles until both individuals feel heard and understood.

PART FOUR: PROBLEM-SOLVING, COMPROMISING, SOLUTION-FOCUSED CONVERSATION

Now we get to problem-solving! The mistake so many couples make is that they start here. We want to move to problem-solving only after each person feels heard. This may take multiple dialogue sessions. When engaging in problem-solving, some key questions we want to ask one another are "How can I best support you with this?" "What do you need from me to feel better supported?" "How do you feel about (insert idea)?"

The goal is to let curiosity lead our problem-solving quest and continue to be open to compromise and getting creative with our partner.

3 STEPS OF DIALOGUE

Step 1

Partner A
Sender

Partner B
Receiver

I statements ──────────→ Active listening
Emotion words ──────────→ Validation

Step 2: Switch Roles

Partner A
Receiver

Partner B
Sender

Active listening ←────────── I statements
Validation ←────────── Emotion words

Step 3

Problem Solving: Helpful Phrases

How can I best support you with this?
What does it look like for this to heal between us?

RELATIONSHIP CULTURE

Each relationship has a culture. Norms, expectations, beliefs, rules, and roles. For most people, there is no intention around creating a relationship culture; it just happens. The times you want to speak up but you don't because you don't want to "hurt your partner's feelings," you are creating a culture where you prioritize keeping the peace over sharing your truth. Maybe the culture is that we nag each other passive-aggressively until we get what we really want. Maybe we have a fabulous culture of expressing gratitude and appreciation, or maybe we don't? Maybe we make efforts to spend quality time together. Maybe we haven't been on a vacation together in five years…

Every choice you make in a relationship creates a culture. When corporations are struggling with profit, one of the biggest culprits is company culture. Just as companies have mission statements, there needs to be mutual agreement on relationship culture. To make your relationship culture crystal clear, I recommend sitting down with your partner and creating a relationship agreement list. This does not have to be scary! In fact, it can be fun. You will want to be super honest with one another about your core values and what is important to each of you during this stage of your relationship.

MAKE SPACE AND ALLOW

Remember how back in Chapter 2, I talked about getting rid of your old relationship couch before you get a new one? You don't want one couch on top of another, right? As well as physical space, emotional space, and mental space, you need to make *time* space in your life for a relationship. So many women I work with have poured their energy into their career, their friendships, their families, and their health. And yet they have neglected their romantic life. They haven't left any time on their calendar for dating! In order to make space for a relationship, you have to create the time space for dating first. If you have not created time for dating, you won't magically have time when you "meet the right person."

To prepare for a great relationship, it is a good idea to make space for a great relationship now. You need to mark time on your calendar that is dedicated to your journey to love. And if you're not using it for dating, then it can be used for doing your healing work (such as reading this book, writing in your journal, meditations for a great relationship, etc.). Once we have made space, we need to allow ourselves to receive opportunities for love. We need to claim it and let the universe know: "Yes, I am open to love. I am allowing it into my life, and I acknowledge it may come in ways that I least expect it." We cannot expect love to come into our lives if we have not dedicated any of our time to it. Forget the cliché that says "love comes when you're not looking for it." Love comes when you've done the healing work, made time in your life for it, and have removed your barriers to receiving it! Below, you will see some affirmations that will help you take your ability to allow love to the next level.

Want the audio instead? Go to www.drmorgancoaching.com/ lovemagnetgifts to claim your free audio download of these high-value affirmations!

LOVE AFFIRMATIONS

I am more than enough.

I am deserving of love.

I am worthy of feeling loved and valued.

Love works out for me.

I am a high-value partner.

People are thrilled to date me.

I am hot, sexy, and confident, and potential partners are deeply attracted to me.

I am a magnet for love.

My past experiences have nothing to do with my present or future.

My needs matter.

My emotions are valid.

My partner values my opinion.

I feel deeply seen in my relationships.

I am pursued by my partner.

I feel wanted and valued.

I am attracting a happy and healthy long-term relationship.

My relationship status has nothing to do with my worth.

I am beautiful.

I am loved.

I am powerful beyond measure.

I express my needs because I deserve to take up space.

I feel my emotions because they are a valuable part of my experience.

I am attracting a partner who listens to me and holds space for me.

I am worthy of a love that is growing and deepening.

I feel cherished, desired, and valued by my partner.

My partner and I are growing in our love for one another.

I am worthy of love that feels easy and good.

I am attracting a partner who wants to grow and heal together.

I am securely attached, and I ask for what I need.

I can self-soothe and calm any fears I have.

I am unique; there is no one like me.

I am attracting abundance of love, wealth, and joy.

I feel grateful to experience love that feels safe and secure.

I can effortlessly set boundaries that serve me and help me live my most fulfilled life.

Each day I love myself more and I deepen my capacity to love another.

EXERCISE #7.2: YOUR TOP THREE LOVE AFFIRMATIONS

Now that you have seen my list of powerful love affirmations, it is time to pick three that really align with you and give you goosebumps. You can create your own or pick from the list above. You'll want three affirmations that help you quickly realign your thinking when needed and help get you back into an abundant and securely attached mindset. Pick your three affirmations and write them in your journal. You may also find value in writing them on sticky notes, setting them as reminders in your phone, having them as your laptop screensaver, and maybe even writing them in lipstick all over your bathroom mirror! Make sure you see them frequently, and memorize them so that you can refer to them in times of need.

Cheers to you for doing the work in this chapter, and you know what? I'd love to see what affirmations you came up with! Make sure you post your three affirmations to your Instagram Story, and then tag me @drmorgancoaching. I want to see your affirmations and cheer you on! Up next in Chapter 8, we will unmask one of the biggest enemies of great relationships, *sabotage*. And guess what! When we take the mask off, it is actually you, yourself, who is doing the sabotaging. How infuriating is that? We have all experienced self-sabotage in some form, and we know it is so painful to look back on. I want to help you avoid it at all costs. Check out Chapter 8 to be rid of the sabotage monster once and for all!

CHAPTER EIGHT

BEWARE OF SELF-SABOTAGE (SECURE IS SEXY)

I was dating a great guy, Joe. Joe was kind, a good communicator, and expressed a desire to build a great relationship with me. But have you met the sabotage monster? You know, the one who attacks when you least expect it? Let me tell you the story of one of my own "abandon ship moments" where my sabotage monster showed up in full force. I was showing up as securely attached, however, this way of being was still very new for me at the time. I was like a baby deer wobbling around on my new beliefs about myself and relationships. I was still learning how to walk and not fall over (aka go down an anxious attachment spiral).

WEEKEND GETAWAY WITH JOE

On a Monday, Joe asked me if I had the weekend free. He said he had fully planned a weekend getaway, and he was excited to spend quality time with me if I was available. I practically squealed on the phone. "Yessss!" Initially I was very excited. I thought, *Oh my gosh! I can't believe men like Joe exist. I am so glad I learned how to stop dating emotionally unavailable men who make me work so hard for their attention. What a huge relief!* All was well in the days leading up to the weekend, and many times I exhaled a sigh of pure contentment with my newfound, securely attached bliss.

Until…

On the morning of the getaway, I woke up in a cold sweat. I felt sick to my stomach. I had a raging headache. I felt extremely irritable. Immediately I decided I was going to call and cancel on Joe. *I can't go like this*, I thought. *I will bite his head off!* But thanks to the work I had done to rewire my brain for love, I was able to pause, just for a second, and ask myself, *What is really going on here?* When I asked that question, I realized that deep down, I was terrified. I was falling into anxious attachment patterns of wanting to control everything, and the fear of falling deeper in love and not having it work out was twisting my insides. Luckily, I was able to practice what I taught you earlier in the book. I hopped on my exercise bike for fifteen minutes, accompanied by tracks from Beyonce. I jumped around my room and physically shook out my anxiety. I danced, laughed, and took a hot shower. And I realized the mantra I needed in the moment was "I deserve this kind of love. I am worthy of a man making an effort. I am worthy of someone who is eager to invest in me. I am safe. I can receive this love." After realignment to my secure self, my headache went away. I could breathe easily, and I no longer felt sick to my stomach. I was able to spend a magical weekend away and enjoy every second of it. Below, I will explain why this happens and then give you a foolproof framework for wrangling your own sabotage monster.

WHY ON EARTH WOULD I DO SUCH A THING?

When *secure* feels uncomfortable, you're not attracted to it. When you've never experienced "emotionally available," it can feel like a turnoff *unless you've rewired your brain to receive love and move toward secure attachment.* If you haven't rewired your brain to understand that secure *is* sexy and safe, you might find yourself sabotaging healthy love. Here's what that can look like:

- Meeting a dreamboat guy who calls you back and texts you consistently, only to find your brain saying, "Ewwww! He's so weird! Why is he so into me? Definitely don't go out with him again."
- Two months into a great relationship with a man who is showing up with all the signs of emotional availability, you suddenly fall back in love with your ex-boyfriend.
- A great guy you've been dating for six months plans a romantic getaway to Cabo, and you desperately search for reasons why you can't go.
- Your securely attached, sexy man cooks you dinner on Valentine's Day and writes you a card with fifteen things he loves about you, and your reaction is "Uh, thanks…" while you cringe inside.

The above are all examples of sabotaging securely attached love. Even after you have done the work in this book, it is so important to stay vigilant against pushing away securely attached, healthy love. The reality is that as the love you receive deepens, your brain's old ways of thinking may come up. Kind of like the more securely attached and in love you feel, the higher the likelihood of your brain saying, "Whoa. Hold up. This. Cannot. Be. Real. Abandon ship immediately!" In learning to embody the securely attached woman, you will have these "abandon ship moments," and it is important to see them as just that: moments.

WHAT TO DO WHEN THE SABOTAGE MONSTER SHOWS UP

First off, the hardest part is *recognizing* it is happening. If you have done that, you are in good shape. Next, it is important to acknowledge where it is coming from. It may take some questioning. Ask yourself, "What is my inner child feeling right now?" Sabotage is not logical; it is purely emotional and based on past relationship survival behaviors. After you acknowledge where it is coming from, you'll want to send yourself compassion. What does your inner child need to hear? How can you support her? Would you benefit from writing in your journal, taking a bath, taking a deep breath with your hand over your heart? She likely needs to know that she is safe, that she is worthy of receiving love, and that she can navigate anything that comes up.

Next, you'll want to provide yourself with what you need in order to realign with the securely attached version of you. As I mentioned in the example above, this might be a mantra, or it might mean revisiting your "Secure You" list. Here's what I want you to know: This may feel rough the first time you do it. It may feel totally foreign. It. Will. Get. Easier. Just like anything, the more you do it, the more it becomes second nature. With time, the realignment to secure attachment might take you a mere thirty seconds. Let's talk about the new relationship blueprint that will support you in effortlessly realigning your securely attached self.

NEW BLUEPRINT

Take a deep breath. This is very important. I need you to know this:

*You have the right to **decide** what kind of relationship you will have.* You have permission to toss out all the models that were given to you. You can deliberately design the kind of relationship that would be good for your well-being, feed your soul, and light you up. Your parents' relationship is not your relationship. Your friends' relationship is not yours. Your parents were not affectionate, barely spoke to one another, and slept in separate bedrooms? You can reject that model and decide your relationship will be full of connection and affection. You can decide you will laugh, snuggle, and communicate openly with your partner. You get to decide. The trick is: you must decide. Otherwise, you will resort to your default programming (aka the relationship models most hardwired into your brain).

Do you remember in Chapter 2 how we directly addressed your beliefs about relationships? You were asked to toss out unhelpful, love-sabotaging beliefs and replace them with beliefs about relationships that support you in attracting and maintaining a great relationship. Well, hopefully you developed some core beliefs such as "I am worthy of love. There is a partner out there right now who would love to date me and wants to build a securely attached relationship with me. Dating is easy and fun, and I can't wait to date." Now that you have some foundational beliefs, you can add to that foundation to design your ideal relationship, and I am going to teach you exactly how to do this. It's fun, it's easy, and it's life-changing.

EXERCISE #8.1: DESIGNING YOUR IDEAL RELATIONSHIP

Once again, grab your journal and prepare to dig deep and examine the following questions:

First step: *Ask yourself how you want to feel in your relationship.*

Example: I want to feel safe and secure. I want to feel desired. I want to feel nurtured and cared for. I want to feel free. I want to feel sexy, beautiful, and adored. I want to feel inspired and gently challenged to grow.

Second step: *Take each feeling and operationalize it.*

Example: I want to feel safe and secure. This would look like honest, open communication, clear boundaries, and honesty about how the relationship is progressing.

I want to feel inspired and gently challenged to grow. This would look like a partner who is committed to personal growth and supports me in my desire to grow.

Third step: *Add your "I feel" statements to your morning alignment as if they have already happened.*

Example: I feel safe, secure, and loved in my relationship. My partner supports me in my growth. I feel desired and adored by how my partner treats me.

Important: et creative! Have fun with this. If you're not sure how you want to feel, make sure you intentionally explore how you want to feel. Sit with yourself in meditation and imagine you're speaking with yourself one year from now, when you're in a great relationship. How does that version of you feel? What is important to her? What does her relationship look like?

Here's a trick to speed up the attraction of your ideal partner. *Intentionally decide to begin feeling how you want to feel NOW.* If I want to feel "desired," how can I create that feeling for myself now, before my partner has entered my life? Intentionally care for yourself in the ways you'd desire a partner to care for you. The beautiful thing about this is that it gives you absolute clarity on how you want to feel, reminds you that you can create that feeling for yourself, and attracts people who desire those same feelings. Essentially, feel into how you want to feel, and the people who want to support you in feeling that way will be attracted to you. Next, I will address something that might be getting in the way of you building your ideal relationship: pesky plastic plant relationships. No idea what I'm talking about? Keep reading!

NO MORE PLASTIC PLANTS!

There are days when I feel like I'd like to ride around with a bullhorn and broadcast: "No more plastic plant relationships!" People would have no idea what I was talking about, but that's how passionate I am about this message. When you hear that, what does it mean to you? Let me tell you what it means to me and all the women I have the privilege of coaching. It means stop giving your precious energy to relationships that go nowhere. Stop pouring into partners who might look great but have no capacity for growth. Start acknowledging that a dead-end relationship is a dead-end relationship, and no matter how much you give to it, you can't make it grow.

A plastic plant is a plastic plant, just as a no–capacity-for-growth relationship is what it is. Here's the deal. You don't fault a plastic plant for being a plastic plant. That's what it is. And you also don't go, "Oooooh, well, if I bought special fertilizer, moved it to the perfect spot in my house where it gets more sunlight, and started singing to it seven times a day, it would grow!" No! You and I know that no matter what magic you throw at a plastic plant, it ain't growing an inch. We need to apply this same philosophy to relationships. Some of us develop what psychologists refer to as "sunk cost bias," as in, "I've already invested so much into this relationship; I will just keep investing more." When we make decisions based on this bias, we have anchored ourselves to past efforts and provided ourselves with no room to acknowledge reality or how our needs have changed. Sunk cost bias can cause people to stay in twenty-year marriages when they knew their partner wasn't right for them six months in. It can show up in relationships when people decide to "just work harder," even when they are simply not compatible. It can look like this: "Oh, scheduling a date night didn't help bring us closer, so let's do couples therapy! Oh, he still doesn't hear my needs. Maybe I need to spell them out more clearly and do a dance while I communicate to him. We haven't had sex in two years. He won't even kiss me anymore, but maybe if we go on a week-long vacation, we can feel a spark again."

Please understand I am not saying to throw in the towel when a relationship has challenges. *Every* relationship will have conflict and hard times. The most important prerequisite to any great relationship is that both people are committed to showing up and doing the work together and that both people desire to cocreate a secure attachment. I am not saying this will be easy. However, if you have shown up again and again, and your effort is not matched by your partner, or your relationship is adding no value to your life, then don't let sunk cost bias deceive you into continuing to invest in a plastic plant.

You deserve a relationship where you are *not*:

- "trying to make it work" by yourself;

- stuck feeling completely alone;
- walking on eggshells/struggling to express yourself; or
- unable to communicate your needs and boundaries.

EXERCISE #8.2: IS THIS RELATIONSHIP A PLASTIC PLANT?

In order to determine if a relationship is a plastic plant relationship, you must develop self-trust and *learn to gather the data.* When deciding whether to stay or to go, you need to learn to "trust your gut" and review the data. Just as we discussed in Chapter 6, you have to be a love scientist. Here are some questions you might ask when gathering data on your relationship and deciding whether to keep investing emotionally or to leave the relationship:

"Do I feel heard in this relationship? Can I express myself?"

"What are the ways I contribute to our dynamic? How does my partner contribute?"

"Do we experience positive connection? And if so, what creates it?"

"Is there anything I need to communicate to see if my partner is open to growing together?"

"What are the red flags/yellow flags/green flags?"

"Does this relationship align with the vision I have for my life?"

"What do I see our relationship becoming in five years?"

I gave you some great questions to get you started, and you may want to add more depending on your relationship and your unique situation. The point is: tune in to yourself and what you know to be true about the relationship dynamic. You must get very honest about the plastic plant relationships in your life. Remember, you need to water the relationships that deserve your energy and are capable of growing with you.

Up next, we are going full circle to where this book started: YOU. In the final chapters of this book, you will learn how to continue to grow as an individual while simultaneously growing in relationships. No more losing yourself and neglecting your inner peace. You deserve to grow alongside a partner who supports the happiest, healthiest, most securely attached version of you! The most healed and emotionally well version of you is also the version of you who has great relationships. No more neglecting yourself in the name of "love." Love is made possible by the overflow you feel when you are operating as your highest self. Let's go!

EMPOWERED, SECURELY ATTACHED, AND LOVED FOR LIFE

CHAPTER NINE

BE A SCIENTIST FOR LIFE

I stood in front of Mark in an Applebee's parking lot. I had our favorite wine in hand. It was to be a gift to celebrate six amazing months together. As I reached out to hand it to him, he told me that he "had something to tell me" and that he "wasn't ready for anything serious and needed to end our relationship." Let's rewind for a second. The romance had been a whirlwind, and our connection was electric. There were weekends away, snowboarding trips, nights spent camping under the stars. About three months into our relationship, I knew I was falling in love, and I had expressed that to him. Then six months in, after a weekend away together, he broke up with me in an Applebee's parking lot. I was devastated. I felt so much physical and emotional pain that I wanted to curl up in the fetal position on the concrete and never get up. Instead, I thanked him for being honest and I handed him the bottle of DAOU wine. I got into my car, and I drove away. I cried the entire two-hour drive home. That night when I got home, instead of reaching for wine, I grabbed my journal. I was on my way to becoming a relationship scientist. This is what I'm going to teach you in this chapter.

REJECTION IS REDIRECTION (OBSTACLES ARE SIMPLY REDIRECTIONS TO WHAT IS MEANT FOR YOU)

With Lauryn Hill's "When It Hurts So Bad" blasting on the speakers, when I got home from Applebee's, I began to journal. I let out all of the sadness, the grief, and the mourning of a future that would never come to be. Between sobs, I wrote and wrote. I knew I had to *feel through* what I was going through. I continued to journal as I acknowledged the reality of our breakup and the reality of the role I played. I wrote pages and pages...my hand started to cramp up, and I realized I was approaching this breakup so much differently than I had in the past. I asked myself, is this what a "healthy" breakup feels like?

Here's what stood out to me about this breakup:

- When he told me he was done, I believed him, and I honored his decision (in the past, I had tried endlessly to "get my partner back" and "make him want me again").
- I allowed myself to feel the pain and grief (in the past, I would throw on my best outfit and head out to immediately meet new dating prospects).
- I did not numb, distract, or avoid; I actively made space in my schedule to process the ending of this relationship (in the past, I would fill up my schedule as much as possible).
- I took ownership for the role I played in our breakup and for his contribution as well (in the past, I would go back and forth between entirely blaming myself or blaming my partner).
- I moved through it so much more quickly. I was able to release the relationship within days instead of months (or years! In the past, breakups wreaked havoc on my life for at least three months or more).
- I felt hope for the future. I trusted myself. I believed this

relationship wasn't meant to be and that this breakup was guiding me toward what *was* meant for me.

After about an hour of journaling, it shocked me that I could feel into *gratitude*. Gratitude for the connection to this person, for our time together, and for the ways I had grown as an individual during our relationship. I sat there in my bed, and I let out a deep exhale. I knew I would be okay. I know that each of you reading this have your own painful "breakup stories," and I know each relationship ending has its own unique pain. I find that while the amount of time invested in the relationship is definitely a factor, the connection that you felt and the story you told yourself about the future positively correlate with the pain that you experience when it ends.

In feeling through the pain, you give yourself the opportunity to release it. And in letting go of an old story, you give yourself permission to write a new one. After a "rejection" or breakup, no matter how big or small, whether it was your choice or the other person's, allow yourself to rewrite the narrative as "I may not fully feel this right now, but this is happening for my own good. I trust that releasing this relationship is getting me closer to what is meant for me." Know this: every relationship you are in assists you in your growth as an individual and as a partner. In the weeks following the breakup, I chose to write letters to my future husband. I chose to believe more deeply in my bones that love was on its way to me.

I could have started wearing all black, going to the gym twice a day, and listening to my "F*ck Men" Spotify playlist. Yes, girl, I know you have that playlist too. It's okay. I could have completely walled myself off and bashed love. To bash love and proclaim we do not want it in our lives ever again is to be so deeply hurt that we cannot allow ourselves to feel. Remember, there is NO FAILURE in dating. You are simply being redirected to what is meant for you. When you feel like giving up on the dream of a great relationship, that is your sign to lean in. That is your sign to grab your journal and get rid of all the gunk from your past that is blocking you. It is your sign to relight your inner fire and deepen your belief. Next, I want to talk about continuing to be a scientist about your happiness whether you're married, single, dating, or otherwise.

QUESTIONING BRINGS UNDERSTANDING

You owe it to yourself to study *attribution* in your daily life. Understanding "attribution" means you can connect outcomes in your life to actions, behaviors, thoughts. For example, "Today was a *fantastic* day! I had so much energy. I felt so alive and so connected to my partner." If I say all this, I could just go to bed smiling and then wake up hoping I feel the same way tomorrow. *Or* I could practice studying attribution by getting curious and asking, "What was it about today that made it feel so perfect? What do I need to do more of? What is going well in my life right now?"

The power of studying attribution lies in our ability to take the data and apply it to our behaviors, beliefs, and actions. For example, if I learn that I connect best with my partner after I have taken a bath and released the masculine energy from my day, then I will want to ensure I take baths more often! Or maybe I realize my day goes a lot more smoothly when I spend ten minutes meditating in the morning. In the same way you become a love scientist when dating, you want to be a scientist about your daily life. The happiest, most on-fire, and badass version of you is curious about what works in her life and *what doesn't*. The beautiful thing about "doing the work" is that you can *become* a woman who honors her boundaries. When you honor your boundaries, you create more time in your life for the things that fill you up, and you "delete" the rest. You deserve to have space in your life for the things that bring you joy! You deserve to create the guardrails in your life that allow you to drive to the top of the mountain.

Part of embodying the securely attached woman is allowing yourself to evolve and allowing yourself to be forever curious about what you need in your current season. It is up to you to maintain a relationship with yourself. One of the ways you can do this is by studying the attribution in your life and then taking that data and applying it. It looks like honoring your nonnegotiable self-care behaviors no matter your relationship status or work schedule. Honor the data, and make commitments to yourself that you will apply it to your life. I want to teach you an easy, practical way you can apply this to your life today. It is called a "calendar audit."

EXERCISE #9.1: CALENDAR AUDIT

Next, we will talk about how to ensure that you maintain your transformation (instead of falling back into old habits that keep you stuck and no longer serve you).

I want you to take out your calendar (Google calendar, day planner, etc.) and then grab your journal. You are going to make three categories:

1. Gives Me Energy
2. Drains My Energy

3. Neutral/Not Sure

When you look at your calendar, I want you to place the events/ commitments you had from last week in one of the three categories above. You will want to reevaluate anything that falls into the Drains My Energy category and ask yourself, "Can I do less of this? How can this be changed to feel better?" For the Neutral/ Not Sure category, you will need to gather more data and be sure to tune in to how you feel next time you are completing these tasks. And when it comes to the Gives Me Energy category, you'll want to ask yourself, "How can I do more of this? How do I make this a nonnegotiable?"

Next up, we are going to talk about regression and how you can prevent it from happening. This is something I wish someone had told me earlier on in my own healing journey, so I am making sure you know about it!

YOU, VERSION 2.0

Jasmine always felt like the "chubby kid" in grade school. She was never taught healthy eating habits, and exercise was not part of her childhood. In her family, food was love. She grew up struggling with her body image, and she just felt tired all the time. Finally, when she went off to college, Jasmine developed an incredible health and fitness routine. She became a dedicated gym goer and learned to eat balanced meals packed with protein. She felt confident in her skin, and most importantly, she had a ton of energy. She loved her new identity as a strong, healthy, and confident woman. Then Christmas rolled around, and she returned home to visit her family. During the two weeks she was home, she found herself right back in her old identity. She didn't complete a workout even once! So, what happened? Jasmine regressed to her old identity.

Regression can be defined as returning to a former or less developed state. Regression can be prompted by outside forces such as your environment or by your own internal experience (emotions, beliefs, energy state). Girl, now that you have done the work inside of this book, we need to make sure you understand regression so that you can beat it! If we do not prevent regression, it will beat us every time. The securely attached, on-fire, healthiest version of you deserves to maintain her momentum and continue to grow. Regression sends us spiraling backward, and it can take lots of time to "get back on track," unless we prevent it. In your dating life, this can look like embodying secure attachment and then suddenly being thrown into an anxious or avoidant attachment spiral.

HOW TO PREVENT REGRESSION

What are your daily nonnegotiables? One of the most important strategies for preventing regression is the dedicated protection of your *internal environment*. It is crucial to protect the beliefs you have about yourself, your relationship beliefs, and the ways in which you take care of yourself. Daily nonnegotiables need to include practices that align you with the most secure and healed version of you. Remember, if you do not give to yourself, how can you expect to give to the world? By maintaining your energy state—by prioritizing yourself—you create a buffer to the outside world. Do not neglect your "morning alignment" practice. In the years I have practiced my morning alignment, there have been days when I have missed it for one reason or another. And you know what? I can tell when I miss it for a day. If I miss it for a week, whoa. After a whole week without intentionally connecting to my highest self, I start to not recognize myself.

Practices to connect with the highest version of yourself are required for where you want to go, and they are your birthright. You deserve to invest in yourself so that you can show up in your highest energy and your most securely attached self. You abso-f*cking-lutely, 1000 percent deserve your energy. Why would you give your energy to other people and not give it to yourself? Here is what I've found: not prioritizing time for yourself is not a time issue. It is a self-worth issue. We all have the same twenty-four hours in a day. Maybe consciously your brain has labeled it as a time issue. However, unconsciously, when you don't make time for yourself, it is connected to beliefs that you are unworthy. These beliefs come from childhood, and we spent a lot of time discussing them all the way back in the first chapter.

If you're reading this and you are thinking, *Okay, Dr. Morgan, I hear you, but I actually don't have time to complete daily nonnegotiables,* my friend, you need more belief work. Belief work is like leg day at the gym; you can never have enough. For support on strengthening your new belief system, I invite you to go back to Chapter 1 and reexamine your beliefs. Your beliefs will sabotage you every time *until* they are rewired to support you. Once your belief system is built to support you, your daily nonnegotiables are a breeze, and you'll easily make time for them. Let me remind you: you deserve to do this work. You deserve to make your non-negotiables, well, nonnegotiable.

WHAT TO DO WHEN YOU NOTICE REGRESSION

The most helpful foundation for combating regression is the relationship with yourself. You need to be tuned in to *yourself*. When you have self-attunement, you are aware when you are "off" or when you are sliding into old behaviors. Self-attunement allows you to have early detection of regression. The earlier you notice regression, the easier it is to course correct back to your highest self. I discussed using self-compassion to realign in Chapter 5.

EXERCISE #9.2: IDENTIFY REGRESSION TRAPS

We all have environments, friendships, family members, relationships, energy states, etc., that can lead us into regression without us even realizing it. One way to fight against this is to identify those triggers in advance so you can be prepared to realign with your highest self. In your journal, identify your top five "regression traps."

Girl, I can't believe it, but next up is the final chapter. Wow, our time together has flown by. In Chapter 10, I will give you the practices that I have personally used to *maintain* the securely attached, confident, and healed version of myself. That's right. You get a sneak peek into my personal secret sauce for high self-worth and great relationships for life. These practices will serve you in both your personal healing and in having great relationships. The truth remains that when we take care of ourselves at a high level (Ferrari maintenance, remember?), attracting a great relationship becomes effortless. Are you ready to learn healing practices that will support you in maintaining the securely attached, high-self-worth version of you?

CHAPTER TEN

———

EMBODY A LOVE MAGNET

PRACTICES FOR LIFE

When I first moved to California in 2016, I thought meditation, affirmations, and acai bowls were hippy dippy, woo-woo B.S. I'm not kidding! I was not digging the beach yoga parties, friends who "saged" their houses, and phrases such as "trust the universe," "it didn't match my energy," and "this just feels so aligned." Maybe it was my mental state at the time or my Montana farm-life upbringing. Whatever it was, I was uber judgmental of all the happy, smiling, wheatgrass-shot-taking, barefoot hippy Californians. Why was everyone so tan and beautiful? And even more puzzling, why was everyone *so dang happy?* You can imagine my response when "mindfulness self-compassion meditation" was introduced as a new therapeutic intervention at the clinic I was working at. The day it was presented, I couldn't wait to call my aunt Peggy in Montana and tell her how crazy these psychologist hippies were. "The clinic director wants us to do this meditation stuff; you're supposed to talk to yourself like you would talk to a friend, and it's supposed to help you…it's totally nuts!"

The self-compassion seminar lasted two months. I am a kind and respectful colleague, so I kept my judgment to myself, and I showed up and did the work of the seminar. Then, something magical started to happen; *I started to enjoy meditation.* I couldn't believe this had happened to me. I felt like I was discovering a whole new world. I couldn't believe it, but I felt happier, I was more relaxed, and I had more energy. Most importantly, I was able to get through my day without getting bogged down by the "little stuff." I was truly relaxed for the first time EVER. Within six months of living in San Diego, I joined Core Power Yoga, fell in love with an acai bowl place, and adopted a daily meditation practice. My introduction to "woo-woo shit" completely changed my perspective and *my life.* There was no going back. I tell you this story in case you find yourself feeling a bit apprehensive when it comes to meditation, affirmations, and anything "woo-woo." I get it, and I also believe you owe it to yourself to try it for at least thirty days.

Through my own healing journey, I became 100 percent committed to the version of me I knew I deserved, the version of me who unapologetically chased her dreams. Affirmations played a major role in *maintaining* my momentum and pushing me forward. I proved to myself that they worked, and they worked because I used them consistently. After a particularly impactful breakthrough coaching experience, I went back to my downtown San Diego apartment, and I immediately covered the walls in sticky notes. I wrote on my mirror in lipstick. I hung up two giant whiteboards. My apartment became a personal transformation lab. I wrote my affirmations EVERYWHERE. The best part was, I didn't care what people thought of me anymore, so if friends or family visited, I had no shame. I would smile and say, "Feel free to read those if you like." I became unapologetic about my transformation.

So what is the science behind affirmations? Why do they work? They work because of the power of identity. Reading daily affirmations assists our brains in what is called *self-affirmation*. Our brains develop our own unique "identity." The blueprint for who we believe ourselves to be. Problems arise when we do not intentionally create this identity. Through using affirmations, we can intentionally rewire our brains to create a new sense of identity. Ideally, we let go of lies and welcome in the identity of who we truly are at our core. We rewire to create the identity blueprint of our most love-filled, peaceful, and authentic selves. Then, the important concept of self-integrity comes into play. Self-integrity explains that we desire *to act in ways that correspond to our core identity*. The brain naturally desires that our actions align with our identity; hence, when we rewire our identity, we change the course of our actions.

A lot of people desire to attract a loving, great relationship, but they do not grasp the "change your identity first" concept! Lucky for you, you are here reading this book, so you will be one of the few to grasp it. To further illustrate this point, I want to introduce to you this lovely triangle:

BE-DO-HAVE

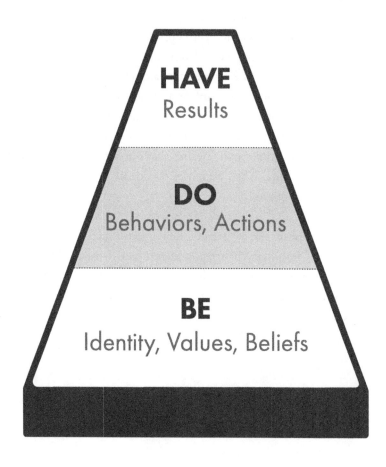

HAVE
Results

DO
Behaviors, Actions

BE
Identity, Values, Beliefs

The power to attract a great relationship is hugely impacted by the bottom part of the triangle, our identity, values, beliefs, and attitudes. Once you can change your values, beliefs, and attitudes when it comes to relationships, your behaviors change as well, and voilà! A great relationship comes into your life. Can I let you in on a secret? This concept also applies to your career, your finances, your health, and every single area of your life. Instead of making New Year's resolutions, you are better served to make an identity upgrade. Resolutions fail; identity upgrades allow you to be 100 percent all in. And more importantly, *they make change easy.* The key is to very intentionally create your identity and change your behavior to affirm it. You already have a huge head start in this area since you created your morning alignment document in Chapter 3. Now you will understand the process behind the morning alignment and be able to take it even deeper. I get goosebumps when I think of the possibilities available to you with this information!

PRO TIPS FOR CREATING AFFIRMATIONS

When we create affirmations, we need to say them as if what we desire is our present reality. You are feeling into your future self when you say an affirmation. For example, you would not say, "I will find a partner." Instead, you would say, "I am in a great relationship with a loving partner, and I feel more secure in love each day." Another pro tip is to use emotion to your advantage! Emotion is your secret weapon for making big things happen in your life. Human emotion is one of the most powerful tools we have for change. It helps you tap into what is uniquely you. As poet E.E. Cummings said, "Whenever you think or you believe or you know, you're a lot of other people: but the moment you feel, you're nobody-but-yourself." To increase the power of your affirmations, use feeling words in your statements. Then as you repeat your affirmations daily, feel into the feelings. This will turbocharge the change in your life.

You will find affirmation lists at the end of this book, and I urge you to use that list as inspiration for creating your own. Your affirmations must speak to you. They should give you goosebumps and speak to the core of who you are. Remember, affirmations are powerful, and they should simultaneously support you and scare you. If you say an affirmation and you "don't believe it," that is okay. You can keep saying it until you do, or you can gently modify it so that your brain can take it in. You should update your affirmation list frequently. You are growing each day, and your affirmations should resemble someone who is growing; as you make your dreams come true or you discover new ones, some of your affirmations will change. "Edit your life frequently and ruthlessly. It's your masterpiece after all." —Nathan W. Morris

SURRENDER

"Don't push the river—it flows all by itself" is my aunt Bonnie's favorite saying. It means don't try to control the world around you. Trust the universe. Believe it will all work out for your good. Trying to push the river does no good; it is useless, and it wears you out. I find myself repeating this saying at least seventeen times a week. For those of us that like to push, control, and achieve, we often get stuck trying to push the river. If you looked at my aunt Bonnie's life, you'd realize she had all the reasons in the world to try to push the river. She is a survivor. Both her mom and dad were killed by a drunk driver in a tragic car accident when Bonnie was just fifteen. Her whole life changed in an instant. On top of losing her parents, she also had six siblings to raise (including my mom) on a rural farm in northern Montana. You see, when we experience relational trauma, loss, abuse, or neglect, our desire to control goes haywire. If we don't properly process the things that happen to us, we spend our entire lives trying to push the river, out of fear. We try to control everything in our lives so that we can avoid pain. Unfortunately, there is no way to avoid pain, and by trying to control our lives to prevent it, we just make ourselves more tired.

When my aunt Bonnie says, "Don't push the river," I know it is from her own personal experience of having to learn this truth. I know that phrase comes from the battles she fought in her own healing journey. My hope for you is that when it comes to your dating journey (or any other area of your life for that matter), you release the need to control. Surrender to the flow of life. This does not mean "do nothing." This means do everything that is within your control, and don't worry about the rest. Show up, be open, and let life flow for you. Stop trying to control everything. Of course, this is mega important in dating and attracting your person. Stay open, be the love scientist, and don't push the river!

REALIGNMENT

Are you ready for deeper levels of surrender? I want to teach you another surrender secret. It is called *realignment*. To practice allowing, you must be able to feel into the belief that good things come easily and that you can, in fact, trust the universe. Please feel free to replace "universe" with God, source energy, Mother Earth, or whatever else feels good to you. It is up to you to decide what feels best in your spiritual life. If performing a trust fall with the universe just isn't quite your thing yet, don't worry, I've got you covered! The secret to surrender is trusting that good things are available to you, and as Gabby Bernstein would say, "The universe has your back!" To apply these teachings to my own life, I developed what I call a "realignment process." This process helps me align with the version of myself that trusts the process, believes in love, and allows life to flow naturally instead of trying to control.

Anytime I notice myself trying too hard, pushing, worrying, or trying to control, I invite myself to realign with the highest version of myself. I consciously invite myself back into surrender. One powerful way to do this is by creating a short prayer or mantra that reconnects you to surrender. Here are a few examples:

I trust in the universe with all my heart.

I lean not unto my own understanding.

I offer up my path to the universe and to the highest good for all.

I am effortlessly guided toward what is meant for me.

I am surrounded by love and light.

Today I surrender my goals and plans to the care of the universe. I offer up my agenda and accept spiritual guidance. I trust that there is a plan far greater than mine. I know that where there once was lack and limitation, there are spiritual solutions and creative ideas. I step back and let love lead the way. Thy will be done.

What would your surrender prayer sound like? Maybe it is as simple as "I trust that what is meant for me is on its way to me." You can be as woo-woo or as scientific as you like. The important thing is that you learn to release control over time and start to lean in to trust that the things happening around you are working for you, not against you. Life is too short to try to control. You deserve more freedom and more space in your life. Your energy deserves to be invested into your passions instead of your worry!

EXERCISE #10.1: SURRENDER STATEMENT

Write your surrender statement here, and then make sure you take a picture with your phone and have it available when you need it. Eventually you will learn it by heart, and it will serve you well in your path to surrender.

SELF-TRUST

When learning to create great relationships in our life, we must first examine the relationship we have with ourselves. Before we can show up securely attached in a relationship, we must ensure we are securely attached to *ourselves*. Can you *trust yourself* to honor your boundaries, express your needs, and self-soothe? Start there. Trusting yourself is *foundational* to all of your other relationships. Do you know how to treat *yourself* with respect? Would you want to date you based on how you treat yourself? Are you ready for the cold, hard truth? *We will only accept the love we are willing to give ourselves.* It all starts with you.

So why does our self-trust disappear or, in some cases, never ever develop in the first place? I have the answer for you, and it's a bit hard to swallow. Are you ready? Take a deep breath. We often lose our connection to our inner guidance system because in order to maintain relationships as a child, we were forced to disconnect from ourselves. Think about it. If I express my needs as a four year old, and then I am punished instead of supported, eventually, I disconnect from my needs altogether. In childhood, maintaining relationships is required for survival. We develop what I call "relationship survival behaviors."

When you feel unable to express how you feel or what you need in an adult relationship, this is a sign that you need to reconnect to your inner guidance system. You need to learn that it is safe to tune in to your boundaries, your thoughts, your emotions, and your needs. One of the best ways to do this is to start intentionally checking in with yourself throughout the day.

SELF CHECK-IN

Step 1

Schedule the self check-in three times throughout the day.

Step 2

Ask yourself:
- What am I feeling right now?
- What emotions are present?
- Do I notice tension or any physical sensations?

Step 3

Ask yourself:
- What do I need right now in order to feel better supported?

Step 4

Honor what you need by taking action.

The beautiful thing is that once you start doing this, it becomes a habit! Slowly but surely, you develop a wonderful relationship with your inner knowing, and life begins to flow so much more easily. And remember, if you find yourself struggling to make decisions or constantly wondering what other people will think of you, that is a sign that you are disconnected from yourself and need to put in some TLC to rekindle that connection with your inner knowing. Remember this: you do know what you need. You've just gotten really good at people pleasing and numbing your emotions. The commitment to reconnect with yourself and learn to trust your decisions is a precious gift that will positively impact every single area of your life. Imagine this, for example: you get a great feeling about a guy you went on date number one with, so you say yes to date number two, and then two years later, you're in a happy marriage. Yes, your inner guidance system is truly powerful when you learn to trust it and tune in.

When you learn to show up securely attached, you will learn to strengthen your self-trust while in a relationship. You can learn to nourish the relationship you have with yourself, while simultaneously deepening your love for another. You release old beliefs that in order to maintain relationships, you had to lose yourself. You begin to release that intimacy, and closeness with others can help you build intimacy and closeness with yourself. Nourishing your self-trust is a lifelong process, and it is one that you deserve to prioritize. Start today by applying the Self Check-In illustrated above. Trust me; you'll thank me later!

A RELATIONSHIP CANNOT GIVE YOU ANYTHING YOU CANNOT GIVE YOURSELF

If you are waiting for someone to come along and "fill a happiness

void" for you, then your relationships will be a struggle. *Every.*
Single. Time. How do I know? Well, because I tried that approach
many, many times…each relationship ending in a dumpster fire.
Remember, a relationship is a multiplier of how you already feel.
Do you feel miserable, lonely, and down most of the time? A
relationship will multiply those feelings for you and eventually
cause you to feel more of those feelings! Eeeeek! Or do you feel
loved, grateful, and generally happy? If you feel good as a single
person, welcoming a partner into your life will multiply your
good feelings. Gratitude for life begins now. Not "once you're in
a relationship."

However, as you enter into a great relationship—which obviously
you will be doing since you've got your hands on this book—you
must remember to nurture the relationship with yourself. We
cannot rely on our partners to "make us feel good." Taking personal ownership over the relationship you have with yourself and
giving to yourself so you can feel good are important building
blocks in any great relationships. You truly are your first priority
because no one can take care of you the way *you* can take care
of you. You are the only one who truly knows exactly what you
need. It is your responsibility to honor your needs and foster
your happiness.

GRATITUDE

The truth is: the reason we want everything we want is that deep
down, we think we will finally feel happy *once we have it*. I call
this the trap of "I will be happy when…" The problem is, if we
don't feel really good on our way to what we want, we will not
be able to reach the destination we are striving for. There will
always be a brief moment of "Ahhh! I achieved that thing! I got

the (insert goal)!" but then, sooner or later, we will fall right back into the trap of "I will be happy when…" *because that is how we are accustomed to feeling*! When that is the way we live our lives, the feeling we are most comfortable with is lack/scarcity/not having. Most of us feel uncomfortable with feeling good and abundant. It doesn't feel safe to us. We have core beliefs rooted in the concept of "hard work" and pushing/striving/achieving. We struggle to accept and rest in joy, happiness, and abundance.

Few of us are taught that to attract our dream lives (and healthy, great relationships), we must change the way we feel. *When you feel good, life flows naturally, and all that you desire is easily attracted to you.* This is why gratitude is a game changer. Gratitude teaches us to feel good about what we already have so that we can open our hearts to receive more. Here is an exercise for practicing gratitude.

EXERCISE #10.2: DAILY GRATITUDE PRACTICE

I want to share with you my daily gratitude practice. It is really, really simple. Every morning, as I write down the ten goals (using my "I am" identity statements that I shared with you in Chapter 3), I also include five things I am grateful for. Yes, I write it out with a pen in a physical journal. There is something so powerful about physically writing it out! With each day I have practiced gratitude, it has become easier and more natural. Here's an example of my morning practice:

TEN "I AM" STATEMENTS

1. I am abundant, joyful, and free.
2. I am an incredible wife.

3. I am a highly successful author and podcast host.
4. I am a healer and relationship expert; I help women make massive shifts in their lives.
5. I am traveling the world as I desire.
6. I am highly generous, and I help take care of my family.
7. I am an athlete and I fuel my body intentionally.
8. I am an amazing mother who shows up for her kids.
9. I am the owner of a home I love; my home environment feels nurturing and beautiful.
10. I am at peace; I trust the universe to guide my path.

FIVE THINGS I AM GRATEFUL FOR

1. My dogs Blue and Son
2. My morning walk with my partner
3. My friends Mariah and Sheva
4. My favorite almond milk latte
5. My twin sister Kelsey, and my aunt Peggy

Now, it is your turn! What are your ten statements, and what are the five things you are most grateful for today?

CONCLUSION

SECURELY ATTACHED AND UNSTOPPABLE

About halfway through writing this book, I met my current partner. I had been in securely attached relationships before, but this
connection is unlike any I've ever experienced. I now know what
it is like to feel completely supported and deeply loved. He is my
biggest cheerleader, my number one fan, and my best friend. He
makes me coffee every morning, he snuggles with me before bed,
and he is truly an amazing partner. Five years ago, I would have
told you a man like him didn't exist. I would have told you that
relationships are pain, and you should just make do with whatever
you can get. Fast-forward to today. I have the most emotionally
healthy and securely attached connection with a hot, successful
man that I adore. We are cocreating a securely attached relationship, and I am practicing everything I've taught you in this book.
I do not tell you this to gloat but to give you hope. You can have
it all. You can have the kind of relationship you desire. You have
all that you need in order to receive it.

I want to encourage you to take a deep breath and maybe allow a smile to cross your face as this book is coming to an end. Give yourself so much gratitude for showing up for yourself in this way! You have supported yourself in your love journey by doing the work inside of these pages. We covered so much, and my hope is that you showed up to the best of your ability to really allow it to soak in. You may find value in rereading this book to really internalize its contents. This will be particularly helpful if you skipped over any of the exercises.

Are you ready to get off the dating roller coaster and move into being your best self each and every day? My sincere hope is that this book has enabled you to do that. We have taken a giant leap toward embodying secure attachment. With all of the exercises in this book, you are now able to take steps each day to ending the craziness of the anxious, avoidant, and disorganized attachment styles that may have previously characterized you and your relationships.

At the beginning of your journey, you learned all about releasing unhelpful limiting beliefs from your childhood and rewiring your brain with beliefs to support a great relationship. You went through some powerful exercises including the "Is This Serving You?" exercise where you took the power of pain to help you fully release your old belief system. Then, you went on to learn all about attachment theory and the four different styles. You learned how attachment styles interact with one another and what each style looks like in action. Hopefully you took the attachment style quiz and now you feel confident in your understanding of attachment theory and your own unique attachment style. From there, you learned how to show up securely attached when dating, and you learned all of the mindset shifts and powerful strategies of the securely attached woman. You are beyond ready to get out there and put it all into practice, girl.

Make the commitment now, before you set this book down, that you will continue to support yourself on your path. Remind yourself that you are enough as you are and that there are so many people out there right now who would be thrilled to build a great partnership with you. Love is abundant and available. Remind yourself that you always have the power to rewire your brain for love, no matter your past. Know that showing up as a securely attached, confident woman *is* available to you. Please know that you are fully equipped to enjoy dating and succeed in finding love. Of course, should you find yourself needing more support and accountability, I would be honored to coach you inside of the Empowered Secure Loved program. There is nothing that lights me up more than the opportunity to support women on their journey to high self-worth and great relationships!

Any time you feel you need a bit of inspiration, return to this book, or simply ask yourself, "What would Dr. Morgan say right now?" I am forever in your corner, cheering you on as you step into the most empowered and authentic version of yourself. If I could give you a personal pep talk before each one of your dates, I would! The reality is that after doing the work inside of these pages, you are ready to approach love in a whole new way. Now it is up to you to go out into the world and attract the love you deserve.

ACKNOWLEDGMENTS

I want to thank my aunt Peggy, who believed in me before I believed in myself. And my loving partner RB, who amazes me every day with his unconditional love and support. I'd also like to thank my aunt Bonnie, who has been an incredible support and cheerleader in my life. Additionally, I'd like to thank Haley Huestis, my right-hand woman, business partner, and friend. This book would never have happened without countless incredible people in my life cheering me on and encouraging me to dream a little bigger.

To the Instagram, Facebook, and *Let's Get Vulnerable* podcast community: You all inspire me to create. Thank you for your support and willingness to grow together. This book is for you.

ABOUT THE AUTHOR

DR. MORGAN is a clinical psychologist who has dedicated her career to understanding the science of love and connection. An attachment theory expert and relationship thought leader, Dr. Morgan is the host of the *Let's Get Vulnerable* podcast and founder of the Empowered-Secure-Loved Relationship Program. She has spent more than a decade helping women heal and find love through transformation and healing frameworks. She is on a mission to help as many women as possible have high self-worth and great relationships. Connect with Dr. Morgan at www.drmorgancoaching.com, follow @drmorgancoaching on Instagram, and find the *Let's Get Vulnerable* podcast anywhere podcasts are aired.

Made in the USA
Las Vegas, NV
25 August 2024

94437897R00100